Bib
11.43
2.15

"In a world of cyber relationships—fueled by Facebook, texts, and tweets—the issues surrounding sex, dating, and relationships have become increasingly complex and challenging for teens, their friends, and their parents. This cutting-edge treatment of the rapidly changing scene is a must-read for parents, students, counselors, and pastors. A big thanks to Gerald and Jay for helping us think sanely through this head-scratching cultural shift from a realistic and theologically astute perspective."

Joe Stowell, President, Cornerstone University

"Jay and Gerald have written a provocative book on one of the most pressing issues of our generation—sexual purity. As the authors show, few things necessitate getting to the core of the gospel like our soul's craving for sexual fulfillment. We cannot think too carefully about what our heavenly Father has said. Even where I reach different conclusions from the authors, I am grateful for another investigation of the biblical data."

J. D. Greear, Lead Pastor, The Summit Church, Durham, North Carolina

"Simplicity is the strength of this fresh approach to sex, dating, and relationships. If at first you chafe at the idea of 'dating friendships,' consider whether any alternative can bring greater glory to God, account for the biblical evidence, and guard against unnecessary heartache."

Collin Hansen, Editorial Director, The Gospel Coalition; author, *Young, Restless, and Reformed*

"What a gift this book is to single men and women. Here, in brief space, is clear and closely reasoned advice that is über-biblical and Christ-centered. It flows with life-giving grace. *Sex, Dating, and Relationships* will be a landmark read for many in this generation."

Kent Hughes, author, *Disciplines of a Godly Young Man*

"Christ-centered reflection on sex, dating, and relationships has been a long time coming; thankfully, it has finally arrived. This volume is a must-read for anyone doing ministry among humans."

Chris Castaldo, Director, Ministry of Gospel Renewal, Billy Graham Center

San Diego Christia
2100 Greenfield D
El Cajon, CA 920
D0249394

"Hiestand and Thomas don't kiss dating goodbye; what fun would that be? Instead, dating is revealed for what it is, which might disturb you. The greatest strength of this book is the contribution the authors make toward thinking biblically about something not in the Bible, which isn't so easy to do. So it is possible that some might agree with their premises and the trajectory of their arguments, yet differ on some of the specific conclusions. But all will be challenged and blessed by their wise contributions to this vitally important issue."

Rick Hove, Executive Director, Faculty Commons, Campus Crusade for Christ

"How refreshing! Gerald and Jay have written a biblically based, gospel-oriented book on sex, dating, and relationships—full of genuine, down-to-earth, practical instruction. This is exactly what Christians need to counteract the worldly attitudes and actions so prevalent in our churches today. It is imperative to think through these issues, and this is the best book I have read for doing so. Dating relationships are so fraught with danger that no Christian should embark on that journey without a guide. I strongly recommend this book as just such a guide."

Jim Samra, Senior Pastor, Calvary Church, Grand Rapids, Michigan

"Gerald and Jay provide solid wisdom for emerging adults and parents on an issue of extreme importance in our day. Young adults who wish to follow Jesus wholeheartedly are faced daily with an onslaught of sexual temptation. What's more, they are largely ill-equipped to negotiate the sex-saturated culture in which they live. I believe that the teaching in this book, if lived out, will lead to a godly marriage of passion and purity."

Joel Willitts, Associate Professor of Biblical and Theological Studies, North Park University; College Pastor, Christ Community Church, St. Charles, Illinois

SEX, DATING, AND RELATIONSHIPS

248.84
H633s

SEX, DATING, AND RELATIONSHIPS

A Fresh Approach

GERALD HIESTAND AND JAY THOMAS

::: CROSSWAY

WHEATON, ILLINOIS

Sex, Dating, and Relationships: A Fresh Approach

Copyright © 2012 by Gerald Hiestand and Jay Thomas

Published by Crossway
        1300 Crescent Street
        Wheaton, Illinois 60187

All rights reserved. No part of this publication may be reproduced, stored in a retrieval system, or transmitted in any form by any means, electronic, mechanical, photocopy, recording, or otherwise, without the prior permission of the publisher, except as provided for by USA copyright law.

Portions of this work were published in *Raising Purity: Helping Parents Understand the Bible's Perspective on Sex, Dating, and Relationships.* Copyright © 2010 by Gerald Hiestand (Iustificare Press, Rolling Meadows, IL).

Cover design: Connie Gabbert Design

First printing 2012

Printed in the United States of America

Unless otherwise indicated, Scripture quotations are from the ESV® Bible (*The Holy Bible, English Standard Version®*), copyright © 2001 by Crossway. Used by permission. All rights reserved.

Scripture quotations marked NASB are from *The New American Standard Bible®*. Copyright © The Lockman Foundation 1960, 1962, 1963, 1968, 1971, 1972, 1973, 1975, 1977, 1995. Used by permission.

Scripture references marked NIV are taken from The Holy Bible, New International Version®, NIV®. Copyright © 1973, 1978, 1984 by Biblica, Inc. Used by permission. All rights reserved worldwide.

Trade paperback ISBN: 978-1-4335-2711-1
PDF ISBN: 978-1-4335-2712-8
Mobipocket ISBN: 978-1-4335-2713-5
ePub ISBN: 978-1-4335-2714-2

Library of Congress Cataloging-in-Publication Data
Hiestand, Gerald, 1974–
Sex, dating, and relationships : a fresh approach / Gerald
Heistand and Jay Thomas.
    p. cm.
  Includes bibliographical references.
  ISBN 978-1-4335-2711-1 (hc)
  1. Single people—Religious life. 2. Sex—Religious aspects—
Christianity. 3. Dating (Social customs)—Religious aspects—
Christianity. I. Thomas, Jay, 1974–   . II. Title.
BV4596.S5H54   2012
248.8'4—dc23   2011033919

Crossway is a publishing ministry of Good News Publishers.

VP		22	21	20	19	18	17	16	15	14	13	12
13	12	11	10	9	8	7	6	5	4	3	2	1

To Babyopia, in hope

CONTENTS

INTRODUCTION

Searching for Clarity

As he who called you is holy,
you also be holy in all your conduct, since it is written,
"You shall be holy, for I am holy."
THE APOSTLE PETER (1 PET. 1:15–16)

The church is in a bit of a mess when it comes to sexual ethics, and Christian singles are bearing the brunt of it. No doubt things could be worse (just read 1 Corinthians 5:11). But certainly we could be doing better. Much better. The "hook-up" culture, so prevalent on the college campus (and now even in our high schools and middle schools) represents a sea change in sexual mores from even twenty years ago. Sex has become casual, devoid of intimacy; it no longer requires even a pretense of ongoing commitment.

Of course, the church doesn't endorse the new sexual ethic. And the fact that you have this book in your hands likely means that you don't endorse it either. But the relentless battering of the promiscuity ram against the gates of Christian virtue can exhaust even devout singles.

And the danger is more subtle than an outright assault on one's virginity. Many Christian singles today lack a clear, biblical vision for sexual purity and relationships that extends beyond a truncated "don't have sex" concept of purity. What about oral sex? Fondling? Passionate kissing? Where should the lines be drawn? Perhaps even more importantly, who should draw them? Has heaven left each of us to decide for ourselves? For most Christian singles today, the boundary lines that quadron off legitimate physical activity from illegitimate sexual activity are too porous to be of much real use in the heat of the moment. It does little good to bar the gate but leave the back door wide open. Surely God intends us to save more than sex for marriage. But what?

That's the primary question we hope to answer in this book.

I KISSED KISSING GOOD-BYE?

The advent of Joshua Harris's book *I Kissed Dating Goodbye* marked a pivotal moment for Christian singles across North America.[1] Based on the number of copies sold, it's clear that Harris's push-back against the contemporary evangelical dating scene has been favorably received by many. But not by all. Since the release of Harris's book there has been a steady stream of "pro-dating" backlashes.[2] Those critical of Harris's conclusions (perhaps some of our readers) decry what they perceive to be a simplistic approach to biblical interpretation and an anti-creational view of human sexuality. In particular Harris's no kissing policy has often come under fire. Does the Bible really teach no kissing before marriage? As one critic put it, such stringent conclusions rely on "decontexualized Pauline pronouncements" (i.e., taking the Bible out of context) and, if not handled carefully, can lead to a modern form of legalism.[3] Further, many of these writers are questioning what is perceived to be a fear-based, unhealthy suppression of human sexuality. Better to explore the possibility of marriage, they argue, in a relationship that celebrates romantic love and human sexuality than in one based on rules and limits.

Whether the critiques of Harris's book are fair, the concerns are legitimate. Whatever we conclude about sexual propriety, it's clear that sex is glorious and full of God-exalting potential. Any approach to sexual standards that views sex as an evil to be avoided, rather than a gift to be celebrated, misses the mark and fails to capture the scriptural ideal. Further, we must not overreach when it comes to establishing scriptural boundaries regarding premarital sexual conduct. Teaching from our own experience is fine, but we must not impose our views upon others in areas where the Bible remains silent.

But God has not been as silent on this issue, as many might think. If you're searching for a biblical, robust view of relationships and purity, let us invite you on a journey—a journey into the heart of purity and the image of God. We will not be searching for an empty moralism—a pharisaical, legalistic list of do's and don'ts. We will not be seeking after an outward obedience devoid of heartfelt submission. We will not be looking to set up mechanisms for self-control as though self-control were an end to itself. On this journey we will be searching for the heart of God, expressed fully in the person of Christ. We will be searching for a Son-exalting purity that is not defined by what it isn't but by what it *is*. Ultimately—though perhaps you didn't realize it—we will be searching for the gospel.

As we hope to show, sex, dating, and relationships find their ultimate meaning in the relationship between Jesus and his people; the former testify to the latter. In other words, sex and relationships are all about the gospel. To miss this central truth, we believe, is not only to miss the whole point of romance and sexuality but also to confuse God's clear boundaries regarding sexual activity between unmarried men and women.

SOME INITIAL ITEMS OF HOUSEKEEPING BEFORE WE BEGIN

But before you dive headlong into this book, we should probably give you a heads-up about a few things. First, this book does not intend to be a comprehensive book on all things "dating." Though two chapters of this book address the subject of dating (and chapter 7 offers an alternative to contemporary models of dating), the focus of this book is not really about dating, courtship, or how to find a spouse. We have intentionally limited ourselves to the simple aim of clarifying and applying the Bible's teaching on sexual purity. We touch upon these other topics only as they relate to this central aim. So if you're looking for a list of "The Ten Best First Dates," this isn't that book.

Second, unlike many books on sexual purity, this book does not contain a host of data carefully detailing the repercussions of sexual immorality. An approach to sexual purity that uses the fear of STDs, unwanted pregnancies, and emotional scars as a means of motivating singles to remain sexually pure is based upon the faulty assumption that God's commands exist solely for our own protection. Though it is true that God's commands do often protect us from harm (though not always), Scripture makes quite clear that God's commands are not about what works best for us but about what brings him the most glory. Consequently we will not be relying on the fear factor as we seek to help you strive for a life of purity.

Third, we know many of you come to this book with past regrets. For some of you, you've never been in a relationship that wasn't compromised by sexual sin. It's not our intent to riddle you with guilt. What we offer here is a fresh start. Grace never asks you to go back in time and undo what can't be undone. It calls you to trust Christ as the one who is what you are not, the one who did what you could not, and the one who will help you become what you could never be on your own. For those wrestling against the stranglehold of regret, we hope this book will unleash in you a hunger for the grace-filled freedom of biblical purity. In fact, as we unpack the connection between purity, sex, and the image of the gospel, you will see that purity is all about grace.

Fourth, it's not lost on us that many singles today have children of their own or are heavily involved in the lives of children (serving in your church's junior high ministry, etc.). Much of what we are going to commend in this book is best learned intuitively and organically through a process of teaching and modeling that begins in childhood. So, if you read this book and you find yourself agreeing with its conclusions, we encourage you to think about how you can be an agent of change in the lives of others, particularly younger children who are looking to you for guidance and leadership in this area. How much better it is to grow the tree straight when it is young than try to straighten a bent tree when it is old. It's our prayer that through this book—its being both read and modeled—God's perspective on sex and purity will once again become normative for the church.

And finally, if this book is to be of any value to you, you must be committed to letting the Bible speak louder than the buzzing background noise of our contemporary evangelical subculture. We're going to be frank here: what we're commending does not fit neatly into the mainstream culture of the church, much less the wider secular culture. But while our perspective is a bit out of step with cultural norms, what we offer here is clear, biblical, and life giving. So gin up your moral courage and press on. We don't believe you'll be disappointed.

CONCLUSION

For too long the church's fuzzy thinking has allowed singles to wander aimlessly in their search for sexual purity. The road is long—longer than when previous generations had to travel it. It is wrought with pitfalls and moral hazards that threaten destruction and death, both literally and spiritually. Yet the fact that you have this book in your hands is an indication that you long to see your life track along the path God has ordained. God longs for this as well, and he promises a good return for your investment of faith.

We may not be right about everything we've written (but who writes a book if he thinks he is wrong?). Regardless, it is our prayer that God will use at least some of what we have written here to help clarify the Bible's teaching on sex, relationships, and purity—that the glory and image of the gospel might be seen ever more clearly in the lives of Christian singles. May he turn our very gray world of subjectivity into a black-and-white world of Christ-honoring, grace-filled, sexual purity!

1

SEX AND THE GOSPEL

Portraying Our Union with the Divine Nature

[Christ is] united to you by a spiritual union,
so close as to be fitly represented by the union of
the wife to the husband.
JONATHAN EDWARDS

Adam, . . . a type of Him who was to come.
THE APOSTLE PAUL (ROM. 5:14 NASB)

On the whole, human beings are fascinated with sex—men and women, young and old, Christians, atheists, and everyone in between. In all cultures, throughout all of history, sexual desire has been one of the greatest motivators of the human will. Men and women throw away their families, houses, money, and land in order to be sexually satisfied. Some are addicted to it. Wars have been fought over it. We compose songs about it, make movies about it, and write stories about it. And this preoccupation with sex is not simply a facet of our fallen nature. Even one whole book of the Bible (the Song of Solomon) is dedicated to celebrating the sexual relationship between the husband and wife.

But have you ever wondered why all the fuss? Why did God create us as sexual people in the first place? We remember learning in science class about the asexual reproduction of single-celled organisms and being grateful that God had chosen a different method of reproduction for humans. The thought of mitosis didn't (and still doesn't) sound as appealing as the method of reproduction that God gave us. We suspect you agree. But why did God choose to create us as sexual beings? He was obviously not tied to a need for sexual reproduction in order to propagate the species. He just as easily could have created humans as asexual creatures that reproduce like amoebas.

Until we understand why God created sex, we will never sufficiently make sense of his commands regarding sexual purity, for his commands always relate to his purposes. So to establish a biblical understanding of sexual purity, this chapter is dedicated to capturing a biblical understanding of sex itself.

LAYING THE FOUNDATION: UNDERSTANDING THE PURPOSE OF SEX

The primary reason that many of us do not adequately understand sex is that many of us do not adequately understand how sex relates to the gospel. You read that right: sex and the gospel are intrinsically linked. In fact, to understand one is to make sense of the other.

Shocking though this may seem, Scripture expressly states that God created sex to serve as a living portrait of the life-changing spiritual union that believers have with God through Christ. Understanding how sex serves this function is absolutely essential for understanding not only why God created us as sexual beings but also why God commands what he does regarding sexual purity. Ultimately, we will discover that God created the physical oneness of sex to serve as a visible image, or *type*, of the spiritual union that exists between Christ and the church. Though it may seem at first that we are diverging far from the primary topic of sexual purity, you will quickly see the relevance of our discussion.

TYPES IN THE BIBLE

Many of history's greatest theologians built their theology around the idea that the image of God and his purposes could be seen in all facets of human existence. Jonathan Edwards and Augustine were two such theologians. Both men believed God created all of life to serve as visible portraits of invisible realities. To see the love between a father and his son, for example, was to see a reflection of the love between God the Father and God the Son. To see the destruction caused by fire was to see a picture of the wrath of God. To see the creativity of an artist was to see a reflection of the creativity of God.[1]

Seeing earthly entities as pictures of divine realities is readily affirmed in much of Scripture. Romans 5:14, for example, describes Adam as a *type* of Christ. The word *type* comes from the Greek word *tupos,* which literally means "blow" or "impression" and refers to the indentation a hammer creates after it strikes wood or metal. Just as an indentation represents that which made it, so too a type points to, or represents, something other than itself. Often translated in the New Testament as "example," a biblical type is a model or image of Christ and his redemptive work. Adam, then, is a shadow, or an image of Christ. Just as Adam's choice in the garden of Eden had ramifications for his posterity, so too Christ's choice in the garden of Gethsemane had ramifications for his posterity. Thus Adam's existence and actions point us toward that which he represents—namely, Christ and his redemptive work.

Perhaps the clearest example of a type found in the Bible is that of the Passover lamb. A brief recounting of the story of the Passover (found in Exodus 11–12) will help us get a clear sense of how types function in Scripture. As you may recall, the children of Israel spent some time in the land of Egypt. Things were not going particularly well (slavery, oppression, forced infanticide), and so God raised up Moses to lead the people out of Egypt and into the land of promise.

To outfit him for the task, Moses was granted the ability to perform great and wondrous plagues that were intended to persuade Pharaoh to release the Israelites. Moses confronted Pharaoh, who refused to cooperate, and so plague after plague washed over the land of Egypt. Finally, the Lord told Moses that a final plague was needed—the death of every firstborn son in the land of Egypt—and that with this plague Pharaoh would relent. But this plague was to be different. God would no longer work indirectly through Moses. This plague would be carried out by God himself (Ex. 11:4). Good news, on one hand, but troubling on the other. People of God or not, the Israelites were no better prepared to face a holy God than were the Egyptians. Ironically, they were in need of being delivered from their Deliverer. And so God instructed them to sacrifice a lamb and to take the blood of the lamb and paint it over the door posts of the house.

> I will pass through the land of Egypt that night, and I will strike all the firstborn in the land of Egypt, both man and beast; and on all the gods of Egypt I will execute judgments: I am the LORD. The blood shall be a sign for you, on the houses where you are. And when I see the blood, I will pass over you, and no plague will befall you to destroy you, when I strike the land of Egypt. (Ex. 12:12–13)

And so it happened. The wrath of God fell upon the land of Egypt, but the Israelites were spared from God's just judgment through the blood of the lamb and delivered out of the bondage of Pharaoh's slavery into the land of promise. The typological implications are evident. Just as the children of Israel were delivered through the blood of a lamb, so too we are spared from God's just judgment through the blood of Christ and are delivered out of the bondage of sin's slavery into the heavenly land of promise.

And of great significance for our purposes is the divine intent in all of this. The similarities between the death of the Passover lamb and the death of Christ are no mere happy coincidence.

The children of Israel were instructed by the Lord to celebrate the Passover meal every year as an ongoing reminder of their deliverance from Egypt. But what they didn't know was that the meal also pointed forward—forward to the day when the true Passover Lamb would come. The celebration of the Passover lamb, was, we now see, not really about deliverance from a temporal tyrant. No, it was most fundamentally about Christ. The death of the Passover lamb was a divinely instituted foreshadowing of Christ's redemptive work. Jesus himself, while celebrating the Passover meal with his disciples, connected his pending death with the death of the Passover lamb (Matt. 26:28). And John the Baptist, upon seeing Jesus at his baptism, proclaimed, "Behold, the Lamb of God, who takes away the sin of the world" (John 1:29). And most explicitly, the apostle Paul declared Christ to be "our Passover lamb" (1 Cor. 5:7).

Thus a type serves as a prophetic pointer toward a deeper heavenly reality. Scripture is replete with such analogies. Hebrews 11:19 refers to Isaac as a type of Christ, for just as Abraham received him back from certain death, so we too have received Christ back from the dead. The priesthood of Melchizedek, the ancient priest-king of Jerusalem, was a picture of the eternal priesthood of Christ. In Galatians Paul uses the two sons of Abraham, Isaac and Ishmael, as representatives of two contrasting covenants (the new and the old). And, as we will see from Scripture, just as the Passover lamb of the Old Testament served as a type, or foreshadowing, of Christ's redemptive sacrifice, so also sex was created by God to serve as a living witness to the gospel. In other words, when we think of sex, we should ultimately think of the gospel.

Perhaps some of you are already thinking, "I've heard that the marriage relationship reflects Christ and the church, but the act of sex itself? Really?"

Really. Let's dive into a key text.

FOR THIS REASON

Ephesians 5:24–32 pointedly describes the sexual relationship within marriage as an image of the spiritual relationship between Christ and the church. As you read the passage, note carefully the significance of the last sentence (v. 32) within its context:[2]

> Now as the church submits to Christ, so also wives should submit in everything to their husbands. Husbands, love your wives, as Christ loved the church and gave himself up for her, that he might sanctify her, having cleansed her by the washing of water with the word, so that he might present the church to himself in splendor, without spot or wrinkle or any such thing, that she might be holy and without blemish. In the same way husbands should love their wives as their own bodies. He who loves his wife loves himself. For no one ever hated his own flesh, but nourishes and cherishes it, just as Christ does the church, because we are members of his body. "Therefore a man shall leave his father and mother and hold fast to his wife, and the two shall become one flesh." *This mystery is profound, and I am saying that it refers to Christ and the church.*

In this passage Paul is discussing the relational dynamics of Christian marriage. And as he gives instruction to husbands and wives about how they are to treat one other, he draws a tight parallel between human marriage and Christ's relationship with the church. The way Christ treats the church, Paul tells us, serves as the pattern for the way in which a husband is to treat his wife. And the way the church relates to Christ is the way a wife is to relate to her husband. But why is this? By what logic does Paul ask husbands and wives to relate to one another as Christ and the church? The answer is found in verse 32. Human marriage, Paul tells us, "refers to Christ and the church."[3] In other words, marriage is a type of Christ's relationship to the church. Drawing upon the ancient marriage formula of Genesis 2:24, Paul reveals a mystery (i.e., a previously hidden truth): sexual oneness within marriage was created by God to serve as a foreshadowing of the spiritual oneness that would exist between Christ and his church. As the great church father Augustine once wrote, "It is of Christ and the Church that it is most truly said, 'the two shall be one flesh.'"

From Paul's comments in Ephesians we can see that when a man and a woman come together sexually, in some mysterious way they become one in their flesh (see also 1 Cor. 6:16). Something profound occurs through sexual intercourse. The marriage union is not simply a legal union or a social union, a financial union or a familial union, but rather a union of bodies, a sharing of physical life. Through sex, two people are joined together in the deepest and most wonderful way—so much so that they are said to become one. This is why sexual intercourse is rightly said to "consummate" a marriage.

Marriage is more than sex, but it's not less than sex. In fact, in the ancient biblical world, sexual union was the primary means by which a man and woman married each other (see, for example, the marriage of Isaac and Rebekah in Gen. 24:67). Unlike today, religious clergy of the ancient world did not *create* a marriage through a formal pronouncement; rather the act of sex itself created the marriage.[4] Thus, a healthy marriage relationship is the living out of the union that is established through sexual intercourse. (This is why a sexual relationship that occurs outside the context of a marriage relationship is so emotionally destructive. The act of sex, which is meant to initiate and sustain a permanent union of marriage, is broken apart and divorced from its very purpose.)

But herein lies the greatest significance of sex—not what it accomplishes on an earthly plane, but what it images on a divine plane. Sex is not an end in itself; it is a *type* of something higher, pointing to the deeper reality of the gospel. Just as the sacrifice of the Passover lamb in the Old Testament foreshadowed Christ's atoning sacrifice in the New, so too the physical oneness established through sex foreshadows the spiritual oneness that will exist (and which already exists) between Christ and his church at the wedding supper of the Lamb. The New Testament's many references to the church as the "bride" of Christ and to Christ as the "bridegroom" further highlight this parallel between earthly and heavenly union. Additionally, many of Christ's parables use the wedding motif as an illustration of his return and consummate union with the church. And the book of Revelation explicitly refers to the wedding supper of the Lamb as inaugurating the dawn of the eternal age (Rev. 19:7; 21:2, 9; 22:17; see also Matt. 25:1–13).[5]

But it's important to remember which came first in God's mind. God did not pattern the divine marriage after human marriage, but rather human marriage is a foreshadowing of the divine marriage. It's not as though God discovered the connection between sex and the gospel the way a pastor peruses the *Wall Street Journal* for preaching illustrations. No, the connection was purposed before the foundation of the world. As Paul tells us, the sexual oneness of marriage refers to Christ and the church. Just as God ordained the Passover lamb of the old covenant to prophetically witness to the coming sacrifice of Christ, so too God ordained human marriage— from the very dawn of creation—to testify to the coming wedding supper of the Lamb.

REMEMBERING THE GOSPEL

Our spiritual union with Christ is an essential yet often overlooked aspect of the gospel. That lapse is, we believe, the primary reason the contemporary church has largely failed to see the illustrative relationship between sex and salvation. A brief restatement of the gospel is in order.

The good news of salvation is not simply that God has forgiven us but, rather, that through our union with Christ we are born again into his very life—we have become sharers of his nature (2 Pet. 1:4). Forgiveness is indeed a significant aspect of our salvation, but we must not reduce the saving work of God to simple bookkeeping in the divine registry, cleaning out our account of sins but otherwise leaving us untouched.[6] Forgiveness cleans the slate, but forgiveness alone is not sufficient for entering the kingdom of heaven.

That last sentence is worth repeating: forgiveness alone is not sufficient for entering the kingdom of heaven. It is only when we understand that our chief culpability before God is not bound up in our sinful actions but, even more fundamentally, in our sinful nature—the source of our sinful actions—that we can begin to understand why we need more than forgiveness.

Not surprisingly, the main requirement for entering into eternal life is that one actually be alive. Jesus himself said, "No one can see [enter into] the kingdom of God unless he is born again" (John 3:3 NIV). A key component of New Testament salvation, therefore, is centered on our connection to the very life of God, through Jesus Christ *via* the indwelling presence of the Holy Spirit. It is when we become one spiritually with Christ himself that we enter into both forgiveness and life. Just as a husband and wife become one in their physical life, so too Christ and the Christian, through the indwelling of the Spirit, become one in their spiritual life. Through our union with Christ, his life becomes our own. We are born again precisely because we have been united to the one who is life itself.

The ability to live a God-pleasing life, indeed, to inherit eternal life, does not stem from our dedication to God or vows of our will; rather, it flows to us from the power of the divine life granted to us through our supernatural union with Christ. The very life of God through Christ via the Holy Spirit has taken up residence inside us. We are irrevocably wed to the divine nature, and human marriage is a powerful picture, or symbol, of this union.

In the end, our final hope of salvation is that we have been married to Christ. When we come to God for salvation, he makes us one with Christ—just as a man and a woman become one in marriage. This union with Christ is the very thing that provides eternal life.

Indeed, the eternal life that we have now begun to live is the eternal life that Christ lives. The sap of the vine is the sap of the branch. Through our union with him, we have been blessed with every spiritual blessing (Eph. 1:3). He has become our head, and as his bride, his job is to present us "to himself as a radiant church, without stain or wrinkle or any other blemish, but holy and blameless" (Eph. 5:27 NIV). And he will do it. Marriage and sex are powerful illustrations of the union that exists between Christ and the Christian, and they were created specifically for that purpose.

THE *WHY* AND THE *HOW* OF SEXUAL PURITY

Now that we understand why God created sex, we can begin to understand the reasons behind his commands regarding sexual purity. Ultimately, God's commands always relate to his image.

As noted already, we tend to believe that God's commands are given to us merely for our own sake. But this is not true. As those created in the image of God, our very nature as image bearers explains the reasons behind God's commands. Not only is sex a divinely appointed image of the gospel, but also man himself is an image of God (Gen. 1:26–27; Rom. 8:29–31; 1 Cor. 11:7; 15:49). We are walking sermon illustrations, if you will. Therefore, since God created us to be images, or types, of himself, revealing his invisible glory to the visible world, it is essential that all we do be aligned with all that God does, for we glorify God by manifesting his goodness through our own goodness. Our glory is his glory, for the glory and goodness we possess is not inherent within us but comes first from him, testifying to his infinite goodness.

Therefore, the ways in which God acts, loves, thinks, and feels all provide the basis for how we are to act, love, think, and feel. We are called to act mercifully because he is merciful (Luke 6:36); we are called to be perfect because he is perfect (Matt. 5:48); we are called to do good to our enemies because he does good to his

(Matt. 5:44–45); and we are called to be holy because he is holy (1 Pet. 1:15–16). Although the Creator's infinite being and actions cannot be equally and identically reflected in a finite creature, the parallel remains valid. Ultimately, every action to which we are called, every function that he created us to fulfill, relates to God's actions and nature. This is no less true regarding sex and God's commands for sexual purity.

God's major intent in creating sex was that it serve as a living witness of the spiritual oneness between Christ and the church. Knowledge of this higher reality then helps us understand how we should behave within the realm of the earthly reality. In other words, our sex lives should be patterned after the way in which Christ and the church relate spiritually. Viewing sexuality from this framework not only explains how we should act but also why we should act a certain way.

For example, in 1 Corinthians 6:15–17 the commands that Paul gives regarding sexual activity are based on the "one spirit" relationship between Christ and the church. We must not unite ourselves sexually to a prostitute, Paul argues, because we have become united spiritually to Christ. But the prohibition in this passage is not against sex in general but against sex with a prostitute. Our spiritual oneness with Christ does not prevent us from having sex with our spouse. In fact, Paul commands this in 1 Corinthians 7:5. But why is sex with our spouse legitimate and sex with a prostitute sinful? How is it that our spiritual oneness with Christ does not stand in the way of all sexual relationships?

When talking about the importance of sexual purity, it is tempting to answer questions such as this on a strictly human level. We might list the myriad of sexually transmitted diseases that can be caught. We could list documented adverse psychological effects of promiscuity. We could talk further about the negative effects of sexual licentiousness on one's future spouse or the possibility of an unwanted pregnancy. But all of these considerations only reinforce the idea that sex is all about us, as though God's commands have only to do with what works best for humanity. Even apart from such side effects, promiscuous sex would still be forbidden because none of the consequences, however true, get to the root of why God has forbidden sex with a prostitute. The issue must first be addressed on a divine plane before it can be addressed on a human plane.

As we saw, God's commands relate to the image of the heavenly realities he intends our lives to bear. Sex with a prostitute, then, is forbidden because it breaks the picture of Christ's single-minded connection and devotion to his bride. Just as Christ reserves himself spiritually for his spouse (the church), so too we are called to reserve ourselves sexually for our husband or wife. The way we behave sexually must conform to that which God has created sex to illustrate: the life-changing nature of the gospel. Monogamy and permanency are vital aspects of this image. Christ is united to the church alone; thus a man must be united to his wife alone. Christ does not divorce his bride; we must not divorce our spouse. Do you see the connection? Our sexual activity must align with the way Christ relates spiritually to the church.

Therefore, the man who uses his sexuality in a promiscuous way fails to act consistently with the image of Christ's monogamous wait for his bride. Christ has purposed to become one with the church alone. Accordingly, singles must reserve their sexuality for their future spouses as an expression of Christ's single-minded devotion to his own. God calls us to reserve our sexuality for the marriage relationship, because it is only in marriage that the image of Christ's relationship to the church can be lived out.

It is fundamentally important that we act out our sexuality in a manner consistent with the image that it was created to portray. We will explore the full implications of this in chapters to come, particularly as it relates to establishing an objective definition of sexual purity, but for now, let's recap.[7]

RECAP

We were made to be like God, existing as living portraits of his divine goodness. Every task that God gives us is centered on his own purposes and nature. Human government, marriage, sex, parents, and Christians themselves (to name just a few) all relate to God's purposes and actions, serving as images of higher heavenly realities. God is about glorifying himself, and the way he has chosen to do so in our lives is through our existence in his glorious image. Like an earthly father who is glorified through the glory of his children, so too God is glorified through our glorification (Rom. 8:30). But such glory cannot be achieved apart from our living out the image of God, for only in God himself is true glory found.

This is why our lives are not about us alone. We are not our own. We bear the image of another, and the ownership of that image belongs to him. And since we bear the image of another, we are not free to decide for ourselves what is best for us. We must not act in ways that are inconsistent with the character of the one we portray. It is important that we live every facet of our lives as a correct witness to the image of God. Everything he asks of us is so that we might be conformed to his image. Put another way, the Bible's commands regarding sex are never arbitrary—they are endowed with great purpose.

So, as we study sexual purity, we must remember that every part of us, including our sexuality, has a higher purpose than merely our own pleasure, for every part of us was created primarily to image forth the glory of God. When we learn to view the world as a mirror of God's divine nature and purposes, we are saved from the dead end of self-absorption; life has a higher purpose than our autonomous satisfaction.

We cannot let such an important area of our life be driven by mere pragmatism and anthropocentric arguments. We must always view this issue through a God-centered lens. You are not your own;

you have been bought with a price and therefore must honor God with your body. He desires your best. He desires your sexual satisfaction more than you ever will, for through the proper expression of your sexuality, both you and the world will have a window through which to see the heart of the gospel. But if we fall prey to the lie that sex is about our happiness alone, we will be robbed of the joy that God intends it to bring. It is only when we live out the image of God that we will find the happiness of God.

Now that we understand the *why* of sexual purity, let's find out what the Bible has to say about the *what*.

DISCUSSION QUESTIONS

1) What is a *type*? What are some examples of types in the Bible?

2) According to Ephesians 5:28–32, how does sex serve as a type, or image, of the gospel?

3) What happens when a man and woman come together sexually? How is this like Christ's relationship to the church?

4) How does knowing that God created sex to serve as a living image of our spiritual union with Christ help us understand the reason behind God's commands regarding sexual purity?

5) What applications can be drawn from the fact that God created sex to serve as a type of Christ and the church, particularly in the realm of sexual satisfaction and sexual purity?

2

MORE THAN A SUBJECTIVE STANDARD

Purity and the God-Ordained Categories of Male-Female Relationships

Encourage . . . younger men as brothers, older women as mothers,
younger women as sisters, in all purity.
THE APOSTLE PAUL (1 TIM. 5:1–2)

Can you speak with certainty and clarity about how men and women should relate sexually to members of the opposite sex? Do you know what God-centered purity looks like apart from the general biblical commands regarding premarital sex and adultery? Are you sage enough to answer—with objective, biblical authority—that vexing age-old question, "How far is too far?" If not, you're not alone.

As stated in the introduction, the question of appropriate sexual boundaries serves as the fulcrum around which this book turns; not because sexual propriety is all there is to a relationship, but because sexual propriety—in as much as sexual union serves as a picture of Christ's spiritual union with the church—is so central to all that God wants to do through male-female relationships. If you don't get this aspect of your relationship right, there's little hope you're going to get anything else right either.

If your experience was similar to ours, you have likely been told that the Bible doesn't speak clearly to the issue of physical boundaries in dating. You were given a lot of advice but not a lot of Bible. But, as we'll see in this chapter, the Bible has much more to say about sexual propriety than many think. Contrary to popular opinion, the Bible does speak with clarity—objective clarity—about what is physically appropriate between an unmarried man and woman in a pre-marriage relationship.

By way of introduction to our main argument, allow us to introduce you to Sarah, a hypothetical twenty-three-year-old marketing executive. She is involved in a Bible-believing church, loves the Lord, and has just started a new dating relationship. Let's listen in as she and her pastor discuss the appropriate physical boundaries of such a relationship.

Pastor:	So I hear you have a new boyfriend.
Sarah:	Yes, Tom and I have been going out now for three weeks.
Pastor:	Really? How's that been going?
Sarah:	It's been great. He's twenty-five, a law student at the University of Chicago, very bright, and loves Jesus, and we seem to have a ton in common.
Pastor:	That's great. Do you mind if I ask you something a little personal?
Sarah:	Sure, I mean, I guess you can.
Pastor:	I was just wondering what your physical relationship is like.
Sarah:	Well, um, what do you mean exactly?
Pastor:	Well for instance, does Tom kiss you?
Sarah:	Wow! This is kind of awkward to talk about with my pastor. (She looks down and fiddles with the heat protector thingy on her Starbucks Grande cup, blushes, and looks back up.)
Pastor:	Why so bashful about this topic? Is there something wrong with kissing?
Sarah:	No, there's nothing wrong with kissing per se. I mean, there could be something wrong with kissing if two people were getting carried away.
Pastor:	What do you mean by "getting carried away"?
Sarah:	Well, you know—doing things you shouldn't do.
Pastor:	How do you determine which sorts of things you shouldn't do?
Sarah:	Well, I guess I'm not absolutely sure. I know you should wait until you're married to have sex.
Pastor:	So as long as you don't have sex, it's okay?
Sarah:	Yes. I mean, no. I mean, there are things you probably shouldn't be doing, even if you're stopping short of sex.

Pastor: Okay, then let's tease this and try to be honest. What if Tom wanted to give you a light good-night kiss?

Sarah: Since we are officially dating and committed, that would be fine.

Pastor: A prolonged good-night kiss, but not a French kiss?

Sarah: Fine.

Pastor: How about a lot of kissing, say fifteen minutes worth, but still no French kissing?

Sarah: I guess that's okay in a serious relationship, as long as it doesn't get out of hand.

Pastor: How about French kissing?

Sarah: Well maybe, but that's it.

Pastor: Why?

Sarah: I just wouldn't feel comfortable doing anything beyond that.

Pastor: So do you determine what is right based on how you feel?

Sarah: Well, I guess so. Every person needs to pray about it and come to their own convictions about how far is too far. For myself, I just wouldn't feel comfortable with anything beyond that.

Pastor: What if you had a friend who felt comfortable with French kissing and caressing. As long as she felt comfortable, would that be okay?

Sarah: Well, the guy she's with might not feel comfortable. Maybe that would be too tempting for him and would make him want to do more than he should.

Pastor: What do you mean by "more than he should"? How do we know how far is too far for him?

Sarah: He needs to know that for himself, I guess.

Pastor: Okay then. Let's say that both the guy and the girl feel comfortable with heavy French kissing and caressing. Is it okay, since they both feel comfortable with what they're doing?

Sarah: (Pauses) Well, I don't think that would be right.

Pastor: Neither do I, but how would you convince them that they're doing something inappropriate?

Sarah: I guess I'm not really sure.

So how far is too far, anyway? If you're living somewhere between puberty and marriage, it's a question full of great significance. I (Gerald) can recall sitting as a young man with my pastor over breakfast and discussing the issue of purity between dating couples. With me were four or five other guys, some who had grown up in the church and others who came from unchurched families. We all believed that the Bible clearly prohibits sex before marriage, but our convictions did not reach far beyond that.

My pastor agreed that indeed the Bible does prohibit sex before marriage, but unfortunately, since dating is not specifically mentioned in the Bible, we needed to come to our own conclusions about what is physically appropriate in a dating relationship. So each of us in turn sounded off with whatever our teenage wisdom could muster. Our answers ranged from "prolonged kissing" to "as long as the clothes stay on." (And before you older singles look down your mature noses at my younger teenage ignorance, I think, if you're honest, you'll admit that thirty-year-old wisdom isn't a whole lot better on this issue.)

I remember my pastor cautioning against the more liberal standards, using the slippery-slope argument, that it can be hard to stop short of sex when things have progressed too far. He also cautioned us against the danger of lust, which can often accompany even light sexual interaction, and he mentioned the need to be pure. But in the end he had no objective standard of purity with which to advise us. Instead he encouraged us each to prayerfully come to our own convictions about what was physically appropriate in a dating relationship and to follow the leading of the Holy Spirit. Ultimately we were left to seek our own wisdom.

The approach Gerald's pastor took seems to be the conventional wisdom in much of the literature we've read on this topic. No doubt you've heard something similar. One author sums it up by stating:

> You may want me to tell you, in much more detail, exactly what's right for you when it comes to secular boundaries. But in the end, you have to stand before God. That's why you must set your own boundaries according to His direction for your life. . . . [To] keep my mind and body pure, I chose not to kiss [my wife] until the day we were engaged. . . . I'm not saying this has to be one of your boundaries too. I want you to build your own list of sexual standards.[1]

But can this be right? Do we really think God wants us to build our own lists of sexual standards? Single adults—even high-quotient, educated, sophisticated ones—are not qualified to build their own lists of sexual standards. We certainly weren't (and still aren't). There has to be a better way forward.

THE THREE GOD-ORDAINED CATEGORIES

Fortunately, God has not left us without a knowledge of his will. Contrary to what many believe, God has clearly spelled out what he expects from single men and women regarding their sexual activity. Of course, you won't find it by looking up, "How far is too far?" in the back of your Bible. But it's there to be seen by all who are willing to think carefully about the Bible's theology of male-female relationships.

Figure 2.1: The God-Ordained Categories of Male-Female Relationships

As we'll see, God has grouped male-female relationships into three categories. Though the titles we have assigned to each category may be slightly arbitrary, the categories themselves are not. Each is based on unique standards that God has given regarding sexual activity. Understanding these distinct categories is the key to overcoming much of the subjectivity surrounding sexual propriety, helping us to build proper boundaries of sexual expression.

THE FAMILY RELATIONSHIP

We begin with the family relationship. God's guideline for sexual expression between blood relatives has evolved throughout history.

As mentioned earlier, all of God's commands reflect his nature and purposes. This is true as well for God's commands regarding sexual relations within families. In early Bible times, God did not prohibit sexual relations between blood relatives. But with the giving of the Old Testament law, God changed that standard: "None of you shall approach any one of his close relatives to uncover nakedness. I am the LORD" (Lev. 18:6; in this verse, the phrase "uncover nakedness" is a Hebrew euphemism for sexual relations).

Today we do not find this command at all unusual or even necessary. The thought of engaging in sexual relations with someone in our immediate family is revolting to most of us. But this has not always been the case. As we look back through biblical history prior to the law, we find that sexual relations between blood relatives were not uncommon. Abraham married his half sister (Gen. 20:11–12). Lot's daughters approached their father while he was drunk and had intercourse with him (Gen. 19:31–36). Jacob married two sisters, a practice later banned under the law (Gen. 29:23–28). Presumably Cain, Abel, and Seth, as well as Noah's sons, all married blood relatives.

God did not encourage the practice, and we later learn that he disapproved of it (Lev. 18:26–28). But he did not ban it until the giving of the law. The reasons for the ban are not clearly detailed, but it appears that sexual relations between blood relatives no longer fit the new relationship God had established with his people through the law.[2] Regardless of the reason for this prohibition, God's command for sexual relations within the family relationship is clear: no sexual activity is to occur between blood relatives.

THE MARRIAGE RELATIONSHIP

A second category of God-ordained male-female relationships is the marriage relationship. Though God prohibits sexual relations between blood relatives, his command is quite different regarding men and women who are married. Within the context of marriage, sexual relations are not only permissible, but they are commanded. In 1 Corinthians 7:3–5 Paul commands married couples *not* to abstain from sexual relations. He writes:

> The husband should fulfill his marital duty to his wife, and likewise the wife to her husband. The wife's body does not belong to her alone but also to her husband. In the same way, the husband's body does not belong to him alone but also to his wife. Do not deprive each other except by mutual consent and for a time, so that you may devote yourselves to prayer. (NIV)

Paul goes on to note that a healthy sexual relationship within marriage is a good safeguard against infidelity. And an even deeper reason for a healthy sexual relationship can be gleaned from our discussion back in chapter 1. The physical oneness that results from sex between a husband and wife is an image of the spiritual oneness that results from our union with Christ. Sex is a picture of the gospel, and thus our enjoyment of it within the context of marriage is necessary as an expression of Christ's spiritual oneness with the church. So where God has prohibited sexual relations between blood relatives, he has commanded it in the case of marriage. So far, so good. The above two categories are pretty straightforward.

THE NEIGHBOR RELATIONSHIP

The last category of male-female relationship we have labeled, for lack of a better term, the "neighbor relationship." And it is here the Bible resolves for us much of the ambiguity regarding sexual purity between unmarried men and women. Following Jesus's inclusive definition of a neighbor, this category includes all those who are neither a blood relative nor a spouse (e.g., friends, strangers, schoolmates, coworkers). The commands regarding sexual purity for the neighbor relationship are sown throughout the New Testament, and one of the most telling passages in this regard is 1 Corinthians 7:7–9:

> I wish that all were as I myself am [i.e., celibate]. But each has his own gift from God, one of one kind and one of another. To the unmarried and the widows I say that it is good for them to remain single as I am. But if they cannot exercise self-control, they should marry. For it is better to marry than to burn with passion.

In this passage Paul is responding to a series of questions posed to him by the Corinthian church. Many of the Corinthians were wrongly influenced by a form of dualistic asceticism, a worldview that pitted the material world against the spiritual world. This worldview considered celibacy as the ideal Christian life and encouraged others to adopt such a lifestyle. In this passage Paul notes his own commitment to celibacy and agrees that celibacy is indeed ideal for increasing one's capacity to serve in Christ's kingdom. Yet Paul recognizes that the ability to live a chaste and celibate life is a unique gift from God—one that God has not given to everyone.

Given the widespread sexual immorality of the day, Paul does not encourage all believers to embrace a celibate lifestyle. Those who have a strong desire for sexual intimacy (i.e., "burn with passion") should fulfill that desire within the context of a marriage relationship. The implications are clear: the marriage relationship is the only legitimate context for sexual relations. What is plainly stated here in this passage is the assumed standard of sexual propriety seen throughout both the Old and New Testaments. Thus, the Bible's perspective on sexual purity within the neighbor relationship can be detailed as follows: sexual relations are prohibited.

Now, we know what you're thinking: "No sexual relations outside of marriage. I get that. But I already knew that. How does this help me answer the question, 'How far is too far'?" Glad you asked; read on.

WHAT CONSTITUTES SEXUAL RELATIONS?

Nearly all devout Christians who take the Bible seriously will agree that sexual relations should be reserved for marriage. But it is precisely at this point that many of us often fail to think carefully about the full meaning of the term *sexual relations*. Too often we limit our understanding of sexual relations to include only sexual intercourse. But is such a narrow understanding of sexual relations legitimate? One is reminded here of a past president who staunchly asserted, "I did not have sexual relations with that woman." Of course what he really meant was that he did not engage in sexual intercourse. But how many of us (his wife, not least) were satisfied with this truncated definition of sexual relations? Clearly sexual relations extend beyond sexual intercourse. Oral sex, fondling, and mutual masturbation, for example, are all sexual activities. Once we embrace the biblical truth that sexual relations must be reserved for marriage, the age old question, "How far is too far?" is easily answered. If an activity is sexual, it is to be abstained from while in the neighbor relationship.

But for the sake of clarity, let's press this a bit farther. As mentioned above, nearly all Christians who take the Bible seriously will acknowledge that sexual activity should be reserved for marriage. And it's doubtful that anyone—Christian or not—would really try to make a case that oral sex and fondling are not sexual activities. So the line is pretty clear as far as those activities are concerned. But what about kissing? Many (perhaps most) Christian dating couples regularly engage in passionate kissing. What are we to think about this activity?

Answering the kissing question is not as difficult as one might think. Clearly some forms of kissing are nonsexual; we kiss our children and our mothers. But there are some forms of kissing that we reserve exclusively for our wives. And the reason we do so is precisely that those forms of kissing are sexual.

Considering an activity against the backdrop of the family relationship is immeasurably helpful in clearing up nearly all of the confusion surrounding the question, "How far is too far?" If a man would not feel comfortable engaging in a particular action with his sister because doing so would be sexually inappropriate, then that action is of a sexual nature and is to be reserved for the marriage relationship.[3]

That we often fail to identify certain activities (such as passionate kissing) as sexual is seen in how many Christian singles frequently use the term *physical relationship* to describe such activities. The use of the term *physical* implicitly suggests the couple's actions are something other than sexual. But passionate kissing is not merely physical—it's sexual. Unlike a hug or holding hands, passionate kissing is clearly off-limits between biological family members. And the reason it's off-limits is that we intuitively know passionate kissing to be a sexual activity. Thus we can conclude:

1) Sexual relations are to be reserved for the marriage relationship.
2) There's more to sexual relations than sexual intercourse.
3) Any activity that is sexual in nature must be reserved for the marriage relationship.
4) Some forms of kissing are sexual in nature.
5) Sexual forms of kissing must be reserved for the marriage relationship.

The logic of the above is, we believe, inescapable. What's more, viewing an activity against the backdrop of the family relationship has biblical warrant. In 1 Timothy 5:2 Paul suggestively ties together the familial treatment of the opposite sex with absolute purity. In this often overlooked verse he writes, "[Treat] older women as mothers, and younger women as sisters, with absolute purity" (NIV). Most helpfully, Paul here links together the familial treatment of the opposite sex with sexual purity. In the context of this passage Paul is instructing Timothy—a young pastor—as to how he should interact with the women of his church, in other words, his neighbors.

Paul's primary concern at this point is Timothy's sexual conduct, as is seen by his use of the phrase "absolute purity." Notably, Paul instructs Timothy to interact with the women of his church in a way that parallels his relationship with his biological family. Of course, Paul is not asking Timothy to treat the women of his church in every circumstance as though each were his literal mother or sister (think of all the Mother's Day cards!). Nor is he asking Timothy to think or feel about every woman in exactly the same way. Rather, what Paul has in mind is Timothy's *conduct* toward the women in his life. If Timothy is committed to living a life of absolute purity, his conduct toward the women in his church must be carried out within a familial framework of purity.

Any and all sexual activity, even when it stops short of more intense sexual expression, is outside the bounds of the Bible's sexual ethic. It is (can we say it so boldly?) a sin. And not only is such activity itself sinful; it inevitably leads to sexual and emotional frustration, which in turn leads to further sexual temptation. It's a perfect storm of presenting our "members as slaves to impurity and to lawlessness leading to more lawlessness" (Rom. 6:19). This is a simple reality that no doubt many of you can testify to from your own experience, and one that we have seen played out over and over again in our respective churches among adolescents and single adults.

But while the slippery-slope argument is viable, that's not the primary argument we're making here. Again, simply stated, if an activity is sexual, no matter how minor, it is to be reserved for the marriage relationship—not because of what it might lead to, but because of what it is in and of itself. In sum, the standard of purity for the neighbor relationship is identical to the standard of purity for the family relationship: no sexual activity of any kind is permissible.

This is a heavy pill to swallow. We know—we were single once, too. So perhaps you're looking for a little more biblical evidence before you completely pull the plug on all sexual activity outside of marriage. If so, consider the following.

CONFIRMATION FROM THE FIRST-CENTURY CULTURE

A good rule for interpreting the Bible is to make sure that one understands how the original audience of the Bible would have understood a particular term or idea. For instance, in order to understand what Paul means in Colossians 1:15, when he writes that Jesus is the "firstborn" over all creation, we must first understand what the term meant to his original audience. As it happens, the term *firstborn* was a legal title referring to the son—not always the oldest—who would inherit the family fortune. Thus Christ's designation as "firstborn" over creation is not a statement about his birth order but a statement about his legal right to occupy the place of supreme lordship in the kingdom of God. In this instance, a knowledge of the cultural context informs our understanding of the term "firstborn."

The same holds true for the Bible's teaching on sexual immorality. If we are serious about abstaining from sexual immorality, it's incumbent upon us to know what the Bible means by the term *sexual immorality*. It simply won't do to define *sexual immorality* in ways convenient to us but foreign to the biblical authors. As we'll see below, the term *sexual immorality* carried more freight back then than it does today.

WHAT CONSTITUTES SEXUAL IMMORALITY?

In both the ancient Jewish and Greco-Roman contexts, sexual immorality would have included any kind of sexual activity between an unmarried man and a respectable unmarried woman. Indeed, the ability of a respectable young woman to find a suitable marriage partner was, in no small part, contingent upon her father's ability to prove her chastity. Since a daughter's contribution to the family was often found in her ability to secure a socially or economically advantageous marriage, a father in the ancient world typically took great pains to protect the moral integrity of his daughter's reputation until the day of her marriage. Thus, respectable young women did not leave the house unescorted, and the practice of cloistering (i.e., where a young woman was kept in the home and secluded away from any male nonrelatives) was often employed.

Needless to say, our contemporary dating practices would have been completely foreign to the first-century context. Respectable young women, even in the pagan culture, did not spend time alone with males who were not part of the household, nor did they engage in even light sexual activity prior to marriage. In fact, respectable unmarried women in the ancient world were, in many respects, not easily afforded the opportunity to engage in sexual misconduct. (This explains why the commands in the Bible regarding sexual purity are almost all directed toward men, who, unlike young women, would have had more social license to visit prostitutes or take a mistress.)

Consequently, in New Testament times premarital sexual activity that intentionally stopped short of sexual intercourse was not common. Put bluntly, respectable men did not make out with respectable women. Either a man abstained from sexual activity altogether, or he engaged in it fully with his wife (or in the pagan world, a prostitute or mistress).

Our point in referencing the first-century context is not to suggest that we should simply adopt first-century sexual mores. Hardly. Rather, the point is to show how the readers of the New Testament would have naturally understood the Bible's teaching regarding sexual immorality. The common word in the New Testament most often translated "sexual immorality" is the Greek word *porneia*. *Porneia* was a catch-all word used to reference any kind of sexual activity outside the bounds of proper sexual conduct. In Paul's day, avoiding *porneia* would have entailed avoiding any kind of sexual activity—even light sexual activity—between an unmarried man and a respectable unmarried woman.

To fail to take the Bible on its own terms in this area is to fail to adhere to the New Testament's vision of sexual purity. Perhaps an additional illustration will drive home our point. Imagine that a man comes home from work one evening to find that his wife has baked a cake. As he walks into the kitchen, she sees him eyeing the cake and explicitly states, "Don't eat that cake; it's for our party this evening." He nods in understanding, and she leaves the kitchen. As soon as she leaves, he cuts himself a large slice and places it on his plate. And then, bite by bite, he chews the cake and spits it back onto his plate. Having thus chewed the entire piece (but not swallowed, mind you), he scrapes the chewed piece back into the empty space on the cake tray. At this moment his wife walks back into the kitchen and looks at him in horror. "What are you doing?!" she exclaims. "I told you not to eat the cake!" He looks at her calmly and says with an assuring voice, "And indeed I have not. You see, dear, I define eating as 'swallowing.' And since I didn't swallow the cake, I didn't eat the cake. In sum, I did not have eating relations with that cake."

A silly story, but one that makes the point. When the wife tells her husband not to eat the cake, she means, "Leave it alone—don't touch it." And in real life she doesn't need to be more explicit, because he knows perfectly well what she means. It's the same with the Bible's teaching on sexual immorality. When the biblical authors wrote, "Abstain from sexual immorality," their hearers knew exactly what they meant. In the first-century context, appropriate conduct meant treating members of the opposite sex in a completely non-sexual way. The New Testament simply assumes and affirms this standard of sexual purity.

Given this historical and cultural framework, we can understand why the biblical authors did not need to spell out how far is too far. They could simply say, "Avoid *porneia*," and everyone knew what they meant. In sum, all premarital sexual activity—even light sexual activity such as passionate kissing—is outside the bounds of New Testament morality.[4]

So wait. Are we saying that passionate kissing is sexual immorality? Yes, after a fashion. But we aren't suggesting that passionate kissing is the same as sex, any more than Jesus, in his teaching on lust and adultery, meant to suggest that lust carries exactly the same consequences as adultery (see Matt. 5:27). Lust is, of course, a sexual sin. And in that sense, lust is a form of sexual immorality. But we don't invoke church discipline on every person who lusts. There'd be no church left! Christ's point wasn't that those who lust should be treated the same as those who commit adultery. Rather, his point was that lust is the first expression of a big sin, and as such, is itself a sin. In the same way, make-out kissing, while not the same as premarital sex, is the beginning of premarital sex and as such is itself a sin. Lesser expressions of big sins are still sins. That was Jesus's point about lust, and that's our point about make-out kissing. God calls us to absolute purity. Let's not put even a toe in the water of sexual immorality.

THE IMAGE OF GOD PRESERVED

It quickly becomes apparent that the standard of purity established in 1 Corinthians 7:7–9 fits easily with the idea that God has ordained sexual relations to serve as an image of Christ's relationship to the church. When we remember God created sex as a means of communicating our supernatural, one-spirit union with the divine life of Christ, we can begin to understand why God expects us to limit its use to the marriage relationship. Just as Christ reserves himself exclusively for the church, becoming one spirit with his bride alone, we too are called to reserve our sexuality exclusively for our spouse.

Through sexual activity in general and sexual intercourse in particular, the one-flesh union of the marriage relationship reflects the reality of our participation in "the divine nature" (2 Pet. 1:4). But when our sexuality is expressed outside the context of a permanent marriage relationship (either through premarital sexual relations or adultery), we fail to portray the image of the exclusive devotion to and union of Christ and the church.

The restraint required to live out this ideal is great, particularly in a culture that cannot even begin to comprehend the relationship between Christ and his church. But we must always remember for whom our sexuality was made. It was made first for the Lord as a divine illustration of *his* nature and purposes. To bypass this reality and use it prematurely for our own gratification is to rob it of its significance and meaning and thus of its true pleasure in our lives. We must not take that which God has created as sacred and use it prematurely in common relationships that fall short of his intention.

CONCLUSION

God's standards are not arbitrary, and neither is his designation of the distinct types of male-female relationships. Each relationship has a purpose within the image of God, and the guidelines he gives regarding sexual expression within those categories are tied to that image. As we act in accordance with these guidelines, our sexuality bears well the image of God and his divine plan of salvation. Much of the confusion that arises in relationships with the opposite sex, even among young adults who take the Bible seriously, stems from the inability to understand and apply the truths of these distinct relationships.

In sum, all premarital sexual activity is outside the bounds of the New Testament ethic. But how is it that we have for so long misunderstood the Bible's teaching regarding sexual purity? We believe part of the reason singles have failed to apply this standard of purity to their dating relationships is that they see such relationships as distinct from the neighbor relationship. Such oversight is unbiblical and has fueled our inability to discern truth in the realm of sexual purity. As we will see, we cannot create an artificial category of male-female relationship that is not governed by the standards that God has revealed in Scripture.

DISCUSSION QUESTIONS

1) What are the three categories of God-ordained male-female relationships?

2) Who is included in the neighbor relationship?

3) What is God's command regarding sexual purity for the neighbor relationship?

4) Review the five propositions below. Do you agree with each one? Why or why not?

   a) Sexual relations are to be reserved for the marriage relationship.
   b) There's more to sexual relations than sexual intercourse.
   c) Any activity that is sexual in nature must be reserved for the marriage relationship.
   d) Some forms of kissing are sexual in nature.
   e) Sexual forms of kissing must be reserved for the marriage relationship.

3

THE DATING DILEMMA, PART I

Why We Have to Ask, How Far Is Too Far?

Personal boundaries are guidelines, rules, or limits
that a person creates to identify for her- or himself what are
reasonable, safe, and permissible ways for other people
to behave around him or her.

WIKEPEDIA

To date or not to date, that is the question. Since Joshua Harris kissed dating good-bye in the late '90s, the question has vexed the minds of Christian singles throughout North America. And, as you might expect, we have an opinion on the matter. This chapter will explore the subject of dating relationships inasmuch as they relate to the subject of sexual purity. It is our observation that contemporary dating relationships confuse the moral boundaries of the neighbor relationship and have a tendency to legitimize sexual activity outside of marriage. Or, to say it again, relationships take the fixed *moral* boundaries of the neighbor relationship and turn them into *personal* boundaries.

Please observe that our forthcoming critiques are against dating *relationships*, not against dating. In other words, we are cautioning against dating as a *category of relationship*, not against the activity of going on dates. This is an important distinction that will become clearer as we proceed.

Once again, let's listen in as Sarah and her pastor talk about the logic of the dating relationship:

Pastor: So what does it mean, anyway, when you say that you and Tom are "dating"?

Sarah: Well, it's a way of saying we're attracted to each other and want to have a special relationship where our mutual attraction is made explicit.

Pastor: But what about the term *dating*? You mean you go out on dates together?

Sarah: It's more than that. I mean, you can go out on dates with someone but not necessarily be dating. You know, just going out as friends.

Pastor: Oh. Help me understand. Let's say a guy and a girl are just friends, and they get together a lot. That doesn't necessarily mean they're dating, right?

Sarah: Right. When two friends go out on a date, they aren't going out because they're attracted to each other. They're just friends getting together for a one-on-one outing, not unlike hanging out with a same-gender friend.

Pastor: Okay, so going out on dates isn't necessarily the same thing as dating. It's real dating only when two people are attracted to each other—not just in the friendship kind of way but in the *romantic* kind of way.

Sarah: That's about right.

Pastor: So let's say two people like each other as more than friends, and two other people like each other only as friends. If each couple gets together every Friday night and talks on the phone three times a week, what differences might we see between these two relationships that would help us distinguish which is which?

Sarah: Well pastor, I think I know what you're fishing for, and you're right. The couple that is dating will have some sort of physical relationship.

Pastor: So a major difference between a dating couple and a couple who is just friends is whether they have some sort of physical relationship?

Sarah: Yeah.

Pastor: What if two people who are just friends get together and kiss sometimes? Would that be bad?

Sarah: Of course. They're just friends. That would mean either that they really do like each other or that they have a very dysfunctional relationship.

Pastor: But why would it be dysfunctional? Why is it bad for two people who are just friends and have no intentions of pursuing a formal dating relationship to kiss each other, as long as the kissing doesn't go too far? What if they just like to kiss for fun?

Sarah: Well, that happens, for sure, but I don't think it's right. Kissing is an intimate expression of affection, and I think it should be reserved for people who have an official relationship. Otherwise I think it makes it less special—it trivializes it.

Pastor: So you're saying that it would be wrong for two people who are just friends to kiss each other just for fun?

Sarah: Yes.

Pastor: So let's say that you go to a church social and you meet this guy there. You don't know each other, but you can tell he likes you, and you like him. After the event he walks you to your car, and when you get alone in the parking lot, he tries to kiss you. Is that appropriate?

Sarah: I wouldn't appreciate it. Even if I liked him, I don't think it's right to kiss just anybody, especially without a commitment.

Pastor: So you're saying that it would be wrong for you to kiss someone you don't really know that well or have just met?

Sarah: Yes.

Pastor: So let's say instead that he asks you out on a date. You go out several times and get to know each other pretty well, and then he asks you to be his girlfriend. You say yes and everything is all official. Then he kisses you. Is that bad?

Sarah: Then it would be fine, because it would be an official relationship. It's not like you rushed into it or were making out with just anybody.

Pastor: So let's recap. You think it's wrong to kiss your friends just for fun and to kiss people you don't really know that well. Do I have that right?

Sarah: Right.

Pastor: But you think it's okay to kiss someone you're dating as long as it doesn't get carried away or go too far—whatever that means?

Sarah: Right.

Pastor: So you have a conservative standard of sexual purity regarding how you relate to guys who are just friends and to guys you don't know that well but a more relaxed standard for guys you are going out with?

Sarah: Umm, I guess so.

Pastor: We tend to place different standards on different types of relationships, but let me ask you a question: Do you think God has a different standard of sexual purity for dating couples than he does for those who are just friends or strangers?

Sarah: Well, I guess I never really thought of it like that before.

THE EVOLUTION OF DATING: FROM ACTIVITY TO CATEGORY

The term *dating* has evolved over time to mean something different from what it used to mean. In the past, the term *dating* did not denote a category of relationship so much as it described an activity. Unlike previous generations, which understood the term *dating* to refer to something a guy and girl *did* (i.e., going out on a date), the modern concept of dating often refers to something they *are* (i.e., boyfriend and girlfriend). In other words, the term is used to distinguish romantic relationships from nonromantic relationships.

This shift in meaning is significant. As our Christian subculture has come to view dating as a distinct category of relationship separate from nonromantic relationships, we have inadvertently given it the legitimacy we intuitively give to the three God-ordained male-female relationships that we considered in the last chapter. We have created, apart from Scripture, a fourth type of male-female relationship. And therein lies potential for great confusion, for when we invent our own category of male-female relationships, we are forced to invent our own purity guidelines for that category. But inventing our own moral guidelines has never gone well for humanity (think of what happened when Adam and Eve tried it, in Genesis 3, for instance).

In figure 3.1 notice how well a dating relationship fits, or, rather, doesn't fit, with the three God-ordained categories of relationships.

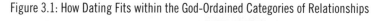

Figure 3.1: How Dating Fits within the God-Ordained Categories of Relationships

INVENTING OUR OWN ABSOLUTES

The guidelines for sexual expression within the God-ordained categories are clear. But we have invented our own category of male-female relationships and then wondered at God's lack of direction as to how we are to behave within that category. Feeling left to our own devices, we then attempt to create standards of purity for this man-made relationship. A dating relationship is more than just a neighbor relationship, we reason, so surely some level of sexual expression is permitted. Yet a dating relationship is not quite on par with a marriage relationship, so obviously sexual intercourse is out. Therefore, we conclude that the standards of purity for a dating relationship must be somewhere between just friends and just married. But there is a lot of room between no sexual expression and sexual intercourse! (And, as we saw last chapter, sexual activity includes all that precedes sexual intercourse.) We have invented our own category of relationship and then made up our own rules.

Here's what we're driving at: the Bible is silent about sexual boundaries within a dating relationship precisely because God does not view a dating relationship as something distinct from the neighbor relationship. Further, the Bible's silence regarding dating relationships is not an instance of the Bible's being silent on dating because it did not exist when the Bible was written, such as one could argue about cars or computers. On the contrary, sexual propriety is an issue the Bible pays a great deal of attention to. While God has not explicitly prescribed the means by which we are to move from the neighbor relationship to the marriage relationship (i.e., courting, dating, arranged marriages), he has clearly prescribed how he expects all men and women to act outside the marriage relationship. Far be it from us to invent our own guidelines of sexual propriety based on our relatively modern way of conducting premarital relations.

BOUND BY THE NEIGHBOR RELATIONSHIP

As far as God is concerned, all unmarried people are bound to the standards of purity he has defined in the neighbor relationship. This is a vital point, and if you are willing to grant it, it will change the entire way you approach the opposite sex. We are not sanctioned to invent a new category of male-female relationships, only to remove ourselves from God's guidelines in the process. Regardless of what we may call another person for whom we have feelings ("boyfriend," or "girlfriend"), we are still bound by the purity guidelines of the neighbor relationship. According to God's Word, we are to do nothing with a member of the opposite sex that we wouldn't do with a blood relative. This clarifies things pretty dramatically and gives an objective answer to the question, How far is too far?

The fact that we even ask the question is an indication that we view a dating relationship as distinct from the neighbor relationship. We do not ask this question regarding our sister or cousin. Nor do most Christian singles typically ask it concerning members of the opposite sex in general. When it comes to such relationships, we intuitively know the answer to the question, How far is too far? But when we raise the question within the context of a dating relationship, we show that we assume a dating relationship is distinct from these other relationships. God's standard of purity for a dating couple is the same as God's standard for the neighbor relationship.

THE DATING DECEPTION

Christian singles don't need to know how to behave in a dating relationship, nor do they just need to abstain from it until they are older, as if age brings more wisdom about how to be in a premarital, semi-sexual relationship. Christian singles need to understand that a dating relationship is, if anything, merely a subset of the neighbor relationship.

We must be careful that we do not come to believe, along with the world, that a dating relationship is a distinct male-female relationship, free from the guidelines of sexual purity established by

God in the neighbor relationship. Nevertheless, so many of us have been swept away by this very misconception, believing that God has not provided objective standards regarding sexual purity for two people romantically interested in each other. God has spoken clearly through his Word. It bears repeating that the guidelines of sexual propriety for two people romantically interested in each other are the same as the guidelines for two people *not* romantically interested in each other: they are to treat one another like blood relatives. Adding the label *dating* to a relationship does not absolve it from these guidelines.

CONCLUSION: THE IMAGE OF GOD UNDONE

Ultimately, God has ordained the boundaries of the neighbor relationship for the sake of Christ and the church. When Christian singles begin to express themselves sexually (even in minor ways) apart from the marriage relationship, they use their sexuality outside of the context for which it was created. God has ordained our sexuality to image the relationship between Christ and his church. To break the boundaries established in the neighbor relationship causes this image to be blurred and confused.

People are sexual, no doubt. And sex is a wonderfully powerful thing—one of the most wonderful, powerful gifts God has given humanity. But sex does not belong to us alone. Until we appreciate God's authority over and purpose for sex, we will fail to make sense of it and struggle to steward it. We must not let modern forms of courtship cloud God's ideal for sex. He offers us so much more.

May we make a suggestion? Would you put this book down and take a moment to pray about what we've discussed this far? Would you ask God to give you fresh eyes as you think about this vital aspect of your humanity? Would you ask the Lord to give you not only knowledge but also grace to obey the image of Christ and the church that your sexuality can express?

DISCUSSION QUESTIONS

1) Do you think the opening discussion between Sarah and her pastor accurately captures our contemporary Christian view of dating? Why or why not?

2) Do you think most people view the sexual boundaries that govern a dating relationship as different from the boundaries that govern nonromantic male-female friendships? Do you?

3) If you are currently in a dating relationship, in what ways do you need to adjust the way in which you are sexually expressing yourself? If you are anticipating a dating relationship, how might you need to adjust your expectations about sexual propriety?

4

THE DATING DILEMMA, PART II

Paper Walls and Unaided Climbing

It's permanent for now.

ONE HOLLYWOOD COUPLE'S ASSESSMENT OF
THEIR NEW RELATIONSHIP

What exactly *is* a dating relationship anyway? As young men we believed in the concept of dating, but we wouldn't have been able to define it in objective terms. But marriage, the wisdom of age, and too much time going the wrong direction down a one-way street has a way of providing clarity on such things. In reality, a dating relationship is nothing more than a mirage, a relationship of smoke and mirrors that promises to be something more than it really is. The previous chapter dealt with the subject of dating from the standpoint of sexual purity. In this chapter, we want to look at the notion of commitment within dating relationships. As we will see, using a term such as *commitment* in the context of a dating relationship stretches the normal usage of the word beyond the breaking point. The fallout from this is significant. As we get started, let's listen in again as Sarah talks with her pastor.

Pastor: I'd like to spend some more time talking about dating relationships, if that's okay.
Sarah: Sure, go ahead.

Pastor: All right, here's my question: What is it about an official dating relationship that distinguishes it from two people who like each other romantically and go out on dates?

Sarah: Well, in the official relationship, the guy and the girl are committed to each other.

Pastor: What do you mean, "committed"?

Sarah: It means they have a mutual understanding that they are going to date only each other. It's different from casual dating.

Pastor: What do you mean by "casual dating"?

Sarah: Casual dating is when two people are just going out on dates, but they haven't made their relationship exclusive. They can still go out with other people.

Pastor: So in casual dating, you can date whomever you want at any time?

Sarah: That's right.

Pastor: But in an official dating relationship, that's not possible because the two people are formally committed to each other?

Sarah: Yes. They've agreed that from then on they are going to date only each other. It's like a form of premarital monogamy.

Pastor: Hmm. So, what's the shelf life of this premarital monogamy? How long does it last?

Sarah: Obviously not forever. Either the relationship is going to end in marriage or the couple will realize the relationship doesn't work for one or the other, and it'll end.

Pastor: "Doesn't work"? You mean when one doesn't like the other anymore?

Sarah: Well, yes, but it can be a bit more complex than that. They might still like each other but discover they have different values. Or perhaps some friction has worked its way into the relationship. Or perhaps they meet someone else who makes them feel a whole world better, so they realize the present relationship really isn't as solid and meaningful as they thought. And sometimes, after a while, things just grow stale. There are a host of reasons to break up with someone.

Pastor: So in a committed dating relationship, either party can end the relationship for any reason at any time and date someone else?

Sarah: Yes.

Pastor: And casual dating is where either party is free to date whomever they want at any time?

Sarah: Right.

Pastor: So what's the difference again?

COMMITTED TO WHAT? COMMITTED TILL WHEN?

Two people who are dating appear in many ways to have a real and established relationship. They have a title for their significant other (boyfriend or girlfriend). They are expected to remember anniversaries, holidays, and birthdays. They place upon each other certain obligations and restrictions regarding who they can and cannot spend time with. On the surface, this does give an impression of commitment. But is the commitment of a dating relationship really a commitment of any substance? We think not.

Very likely, many dating couples have not really thought about what they mean when they use a word such as *commitment* in the context of their relationship. If pressed, however, they usually ascribe the idea of commitment to the fact that they have agreed to date only each other. In other words, a man who is dating one woman cannot go out with another at the same time. He is bound to his girlfriend and has agreed to express his romantic interests in her alone. Thus, it is the exclusive nature of the relationship that separates it from casual dating and other male-female relationships. But, as noted above, the so-called commitment of a dating relationship can end at any time for any reason.

The true nature of commitment with a dating relationship can be seen clearly when contrasted with the commitment of a marriage relationship. Unlike a dating relationship, the commitment and exclusivity of marriage is involuntary. As a legitimate, God-ordained male-female relationship, the marriage relationship entails certain obligations and responsibilities that are irrevocable. When a man marries his bride, he gives up his right to choose any other woman. Prior to his marriage, however, he had no moral obligation to marry her. Once married, a moral obligation is imposed upon a man by the God-given commands of the marriage relationship. Morally, he *has* to faithfully love his wife. The die is cast for better or for worse. It is an irrevocable commitment.

To our harm, we have tended to give the exclusivity of a dating relationship a similar weight. But though a dating relationship may appear to entail the involuntary exclusivity of marriage, its exclusivity is really no different from that of a casual dating relationship. Unlike the marriage relationship, there's nothing in the contractual agreement of a dating relationship itself that prevents a guy from breaking up with his girlfriend on Thursday and seeing a different girl on Friday. In spite of a dating relationship's apparent exclusivity, both parties are free to date whomever they choose, whenever they choose. Thus, the apparent involuntary exclusivity of the dating relationship is really only voluntary exclusivity in disguise. Like a house made of paper, a dating relationship has the appearance of security and stability, but it lacks any true means of achieving it.

In the end, the commitment of a dating relationship is simply the commitment to inform the other person of one's intention to end his or her commitment before actually doing so. Not much of a commitment. Apart from marriage (or engagement), there can be no real promise, no assurance of mutual protection, and no real guarantee for abiding trust; neither party in a dating relationship has promised anything permanent. One Hollywood couple's assessment of their new relationship captures it well: when asked about their relationship they replied, "It's permanent for now." Inspiring, isn't it?

FREE SOLO CLIMBING AND THE DANGER OF FALSE SECURITY

Our intention in pointing out the misuse of the word *commitment* in dating relationships is not simply to achieve linguistic accuracy but to highlight the inherent danger that often accompanies such misuse. Many singles unwittingly depend upon dating relationships as though they entailed some measure of real security, and they are susceptible to all sorts of heartbreak when the relationship's temporary nature becomes evident.

When I (Gerald) was first learning to rock climb, my instructor carefully explained all of the safety procedures, emphasizing the supreme importance of the rope, which would act as my security if I were to fall. This rope was carefully attached to my climbing harness and then just as carefully attached to my instructor. Knowing the rope was present gave me the confidence to climb in ways I would otherwise not have done. Many times, in fact, I would have fallen and seriously injured myself had the rope not caught me. But though I was very aware of the rope and its presence gave me security, in reality it was not the rope alone that saved me from injury. My true security came from the fact that the rope was anchored securely to an instructor who had pledged to stay at his post until I had reached the ground safely. The rope itself would have done little good without the commitment of the person who held it.

How foolish it would be for a climber to feel a sense of security from a rope that was not anchored securely. A friend of mine finished a difficult climb only to discover his rope had been improperly anchored. As he completed his last maneuver, he watched in horror as his anchor pins fell away to the rocks below. Though the rope's presence provided a sense of security throughout his climb, this sense of security was not based on reality. Had he fallen during his climb, he would have been seriously injured or even killed.

In the same way, the so-called commitment of a dating relationship often gives the illusion of security. But this commitment is essentially nonexistent. Unaided climbing is a dangerous activity. Unaided climbing when you mistakenly think your safety rope is securely anchored is more dangerous still. This, we believe, is essentially what many dating relationships are: an unaided climb that masquerades as an aided climb. Consequently, singles are often not fully aware of the danger they face.

THE PARTICULAR VULNERABILITY OF WOMEN IN DATING RELATIONSHIPS

Women in particular are vulnerable to the heartache that comes from relying on a truncated notion of commitment. This is especially true when it comes to sexual boundaries. Most Christian women will not enter into a physical relationship with a man unless he commits himself to being her boyfriend (though even this standard is increasingly falling by the wayside). Because of the perception of security afforded by a dating relationship, a woman is inclined to give herself away sexually (even when this stops short of intercourse) in ways that she would otherwise not do with other men that she might be attracted to. But when we understand the true nature of commitment within a dating relationship, we see that this giving of herself is misguided and is based on a false sense of safety. At the end of the day, her boyfriend is no more committed to her than any other guy who likes her.

In many ways, a dating relationship has everything going for the man and nothing for the woman. The woman gives up the most valuable part of herself only to receive an illusion of security. No doubt many of our female readers can testify to the pain and heartache that came from giving themselves away to men who had made no real promises. As one counselor noted about a distraught woman he was counseling, "She's going through the pain of a divorce and she's never been married." So very sad. As pastors, we have heard this song played over and over again.

A friend of ours told us of his feelings just prior to ending a dating relationship with his girlfriend. "I dreaded doing it," he said. "I felt like I was betraying her trust in me." And, in fact, this is how his girlfriend felt when he finally did break up with her. That both would acknowledge the legitimacy of breaking up yet feel a sense of betrayal (as though a trust was being broken) indicates that we are confused about the nature of commitment within dating relationships. We seem to be unknowingly talking out of both sides of our mouths, using words such as *commitment* and *trust* while at the same time acknowledging the freedom to break that commitment and trust at any time, for any reason.

On the surface, most women realize *intellectually* that the commitment of a dating relationship is only temporary. But they begin to respond *emotionally* as though the relationship really did entail some measure of permanency; as though the commitment of a dating relationship was somewhere between the noncommitment of just friends and the total commitment of marriage. But either a man is committed to a woman, or he is not. Being temporarily committed is essentially no different from being uncommitted.

In years gone by, a man would court a woman to be his wife. But in our day, a man courts a woman to be his girlfriend. How lame is that? Women are left holding the short end of the stick, giving away their hearts to men who have not yet declared their intentions and in most cases don't even know what their intentions are. In our public teaching on this topic, we frequently tell women, "Don't give your heart away until you know what he plans to do with it." And we tell the men, "Stop being irresponsible. Don't try to win a woman's heart unless you plan on keeping it." So women, please listen up: a man has nothing permanent to offer you apart from a marriage proposal. Don't settle for second rate!

CONFUSING ATTRACTION WITH COMMITMENT

Ultimately we believe many singles are confusing *attraction* with *commitment*. That two people are attracted to each other today means essentially nothing about how they will feel tomorrow. They have promised nothing to each other about the future. When both parties clearly understand this truth, they will be able to wisely choose how much emotional investment they will make in the relationship. But when we start placing labels on a relationship such as "boyfriend" and "girlfriend" and using words such as *commitment*, we run the danger of creating a sense that the relationship is built upon something real and solid. But all that really exists is a current mutual attraction. A declaration of attraction is not the basis of security.

We know a young man who once insisted to his girlfriend that they drop the labels of "boyfriend" and "girlfriend" and restart their relationship within the confines of the neighbor relationship. His girlfriend, however, did not like the idea of being classified like any other girl. She greatly resisted the idea and claimed that it would make her feel insecure in his affection toward her. But that was precisely the point! She had no cause for feeling secure in his affections until he proposed. He had made no promises. Any feelings of security that she had in the relationship were built on a sandy foundation of attraction rather than on the lasting foundation of commitment. She thought her rope was securely tied to an anchor. It was not, and this young man was simply trying to be clear about that.

CONCLUSION: IT DON'T MEAN A THING WITHOUT THE RING!

Ultimately there is no true security apart from the promise of marriage. Too many singles today are giving away their hearts without realizing the transient nature of contemporary dating relationships. Words such as *security*, *commitment*, and *promise* have no real place in romantic relationships apart from marriage. Neither party has promised to be exclusive forever but only for as long as it suits his or her individual desires. The insecure nature of dating relationships must not be hidden, for it can lead to misplaced trust and unnecessary heartache.

This is why we strongly discourage singles from indiscriminately forming dating relationships without first thinking clearly about all the issues involved. Dating relationships do not provide legitimate grounds for premature sexual expression, nor do they entail any measure of true security. In the end, the real issue is not whether you have a boyfriend or a girlfriend. The real issue is whether you understand that regardless of the label you may place on another person, no real commitment or security entitles you the freedom to act outside the guidelines of the neighbor relationship.

Because we believe our current system of dating too easily creates an illusion of security, we will suggest in chapter 7 an alternative method to finding a spouse. But before we do, it is necessary to establish a solid understanding of what God expects regarding romantic purity between an unmarried man and woman. As we will see in the chapters to come, not only does God place restrictions upon the *sexual* expression of unmarried men and women, he also places restrictions upon *romantic* expression as well. Trying to maintain these proper boundaries in a dating relationship is, we believe, nearly impossible. Everything about such relationships is focused on fanning into flame precisely what God has intended us to reserve until marriage.

DISCUSSION QUESTIONS

1) Is it fair to say that a boyfriend and girlfriend are committed to each other? If so, in what way?

2) What is the difference between commitment in marriage and commitment in a dating relationship?

3) Two follow-up questions that may help clarify commitment in pre-engagement relationships are:

   a) Can a man legitimately break up with his girlfriend and date another woman?
   b) Can a married man legitimately break up with his wife and date another woman?

4) Why can it be emotionally harmful to use a term such as *commitment* regarding a dating relationship?

5) Is it safe for a woman to give herself away sexually to a man simply because he has committed to being her boyfriend?

5

THE HEART
OF THE MATTER

*Understanding the Biblical Perspective on
Sexual Desire*

And, indeed, this is already sin, to desire those things which the
law of God forbids.

AUGUSTINE, *THE CITY OF GOD*

Hopefully it's becoming clear that we must formulate a new
method of spouse finding. But before we attempt to do so, an
important word still needs to be said about the appropriate timing and context for the release of sexual desire. Too few Christians really understand the Scripture's teaching on this important
topic. As we'll see in this chapter, we need to get back to the heart
of the matter.

Scripture tells us that sexual desire is controllable and is not
to be released indiscriminately toward just anyone. This truth is
in direct contrast with our culture. As we will see, God asks us to
control not only our sexual *activity* but our sexual *desire* as well,
arousing it only within the context of marriage. This guideline also
flows directly from the fact that God has created the sexual relationship between a man and a woman as a type of Christ's relationship
with the church.

UNDERSTANDING THE NATURE OF LUST: A KEY TO EMOTIONAL PURITY

Does sexual desire originate from our bodies or our hearts? Can it be controlled, and if so, how? Is sexual desire different from lust? If sexual desire is good because it is from God, when does it become lust?

When we correctly understand the characteristics of lust, as well as how to control it, we will have a proper foundation upon which to build a life of sexual purity. Ultimately we need to understand that sexual desire is first emotional before it is mental or physical, and that sins of the heart can be just as destructive to God's image as sins of the flesh.

Matthew 5:28: "In His Heart"

As we begin to explore this issue, let's look first at Matthew 5:27–28. This passage will provide the foundation for all we say in this chapter about lust and sexual desire.

> You have heard that it was said, "Do not commit adultery." But I tell you that anyone who looks at a woman lustfully has already committed adultery with her in his heart. (NIV)

The Greek word translated "lustfully" in this passage is *epithumeō*, which is often translated in our English Bibles as simply "to desire," in a positive sense, or "to lust" or "covet," in a negative sense. The same Greek word can convey both meanings. Consider these examples of how the biblical authors used this same word in a positive context:

> For I tell you the truth, many prophets and righteous men longed [*epithumeō*] to see what you see but did not see it, and to hear what you hear but did not hear it. (Matt. 13:17 NIV)

> And he said to them, "I have eagerly desired [*epithumeō*] to eat this Passover with you before I suffer." (Luke 22:15 NIV)

The Neutrality of Desire

In these two passages, *epithumeō* is translated in a positive sense, even in reference to Christ and the prophets. So the same biblical word is used to describe the holy longing Christ and the prophets had for the things of God and also the sinful longing a man can have for a woman other than his wife. What is the point? Simply this: desire itself, from a biblical perspective, is amoral. It is neither right nor wrong. It's like shooting a gun—it all depends on what you're shooting at. Look again at our first passage. It could easily be translated in this way: "I tell you that anyone who looks at a woman *with desire for her* has already committed adultery with her in his heart." So when Christ instructs us not to "lust" after another woman, he is simply telling us not to "sexually desire" another woman.[1] He is essentially affirming the Old Testament law, "You shall not desire [*epithumeō*] your neighbor's wife" (Deut. 5:21).

Both legitimate and illegitimate sexual desire can feel the same. The intense sexual arousal a man feels toward his wife may be little different from the sexual arousal a man feels toward his mistress. Though there is little difference in the sexual feelings themselves, in the former case his desires are pure, and in the latter they are sinful. It is not wrong to desire a sexual relationship with one's wife or to desire a sexual relationship in general. Both of these desires have legitimate objects as their goal. But when we direct our sexual desire toward someone who is not our spouse, we have moved into sin, for now we desire something that is not ours to possess.

Suppose your neighbor comes home with a unique handmade rug from China and invites you over to see it. This rug could excite within you both legitimate and illegitimate desire. If, when looking at his rug, you are filled with jealous desire for his rug (after all, he doesn't deserve it like you do), then your desire is sinful, for the rug is his to possess and not yours. But if upon seeing his rug you are happy for him and moved with a desire to go out and buy a unique rug of your own, then your desire is pure. This is what the law was getting at when the Israelites were told not to covet (*epithumeō*, or "desire") their neighbors' wives, servants, donkeys, or oxen. It was not wrong for Israelites to desire donkeys or servants of their own. But when they jealously desired to possess what someone else had already laid proper claim to, they sinned.

The Proper Object of Desire

Look again at Matthew 5:27–28. An important principle can be gleaned from Christ's words. Though we often tend to define sin as an act of the body, Christ reveals that the desire to commit a sin is itself a sin. It is not enough that our actions align with the Word of God. Our hearts must do so as well. Just because we do not actually strike our brother when we greatly desire to strike him does not mean we are free from sin. The man who refrains from murder but hates his brother in his heart is guilty of murder (Matt. 5:21–22). In the same way, the man who desires to commit adultery yet refrains is still guilty of adultery in his heart. Better, of course, to refrain from sinful desire than to give in to it, but better still not to desire sin at all. This, then, is the sum total of Christ's sermon and the manner in which he defines true righteousness: we must not only choose the right, but we must desire the right.

Significantly, we must understand that Christ did not address his comments about lust simply to married men and women. The man who looks with lust upon a woman who is not his wife desires something that is not his to possess. Since she is not his wife, he has no right to use her as a means of arousing his sexual passions. Just as it is wrong for a man to engage in sexual activity with a woman who is not his wife, so too it is wrong for him to *desire* to engage in sexual activity with that woman.

The prohibition against lust is not for the sake of the spouse but rather for the sake of sexual purity itself as it relates to the image of God, specifically Christ and the church. When we direct our sexual desire toward someone other than our spouse (whether we are married or not), we use our sexuality in a way that is inconsistent with Christ's single-minded commitment and devotion to his church. The only time it is permissible to arouse our sexual desire toward another person is when that person is our husband or wife.

Lust in the Heart, Not the Mind

In understanding the biblical view of lust, we must also be mindful of its location. Too often we confuse exactly where lust takes place. Look again at the words of Christ in Matthew 5:28 and notice the location of lust: "Anyone who looks at a woman lustfully has already committed adultery with her *in his heart*" (NIV).

Lust does not take place in the mind but in the heart. This makes sense, of course, when we understand that the term *lust* is simply another word for *desire*. Many people have a misconception that lust involves some sort of sexual fantasy or an exercise of the mind. But according to Christ, lust takes place in the heart, not the mind, and a person can lust without allowing himself or herself to succumb to a sexual fantasy.

The indiscriminate rush of sexual desire and excitement that we feel for an individual of the opposite sex is precisely the thing that Christ is referring to. This truth is very convicting. Even the unregenerate can control their thoughts. This does not require the power of the Holy Spirit any more than does abstaining from adultery. But only a Christian can have a heart ruled by God that desires only what it should. Let us be very clear about what Christ is saying. Just because a person does not allow himself to delve into sexual fantasies about the opposite sex does not in any way mean that he is free from lust. To lust is simply to desire someone sexually who should not be desired. Anytime someone other than our spouse arouses within us sexual desire, we have moved into the sin of lust.

CAN SEXUAL DESIRE BE CONTROLLED?

Many commentators attempt to soften the force of Matthew 5:27–28 by contending that it is our *intention in looking* (i.e., looking at a woman with the intention of arousing sexual desire) rather than our desire itself that Christ is condemning. Thus they contend that Christ in this context is not condemning *inadvertent* sexual desire, which spontaneously arises upon seeing an attractive member of the opposite sex.

This interpretation, in our minds, is neither required by the underlying Greek text, nor is it in keeping with the spirit of the passage.[2] These commentators seem to imply that as long as we are not looking at another person with the intention of lusting after him or her, it doesn't count as lust even if we do end up lusting. But Christ's whole point in the Sermon on the Mount (of which this command is a part) is that our *desire* to commit sin (in this case, desiring a sexual relationship with someone other than our spouse), not just the actual carrying out of that desire, constitutes sin.

Rage, hatred, and condemnation—just like sexual desire—also seem to well up spontaneously, particularly when we are suddenly confronted with difficult circumstances. Yet nowhere in the Sermon on the Mount does Christ excuse these emotional responses because they are not premeditated or solicited. Rather, he condemns them (Matt. 5:22). Spontaneous emotional responses are not morally neutral; they reveal the conditions of our hearts. When we spontaneously respond in rage to the rude driver, in condemnation to the fallen saint, or in lust to the attractive woman, we reveal that the agendas of our hearts are not as aligned with God as they should be.

Let us not deceive ourselves. If we spontaneously desire a member of the opposite sex we have entered into the realm of lust, even if we don't continue to cultivate that desire or follow through with it. We are, in that moment, desiring that which is illegitimate. Better to overcome lust than to give in to it, but better still not to lust at all.

The more liberal interpretations of Matthew 5:27–28 are in keeping with an age that increasingly views sexual desire as an appetite of the body, as uncontrollable as hunger and thirst. Even we Christians have fallen into this misconception. We must not define sexual arousal as strictly an act of the body; it is a passion of the heart. It is true that no amount of commands from our will can make our body cease to feel hunger, thirst, or pain. But sexual desire is more than just a bodily appetite. The fact that we are told to control it is a clear indication that we can, in fact, control it (see Song 2:7). Christ's commands would be essentially meaningless if this were not the case.

WHO CONTROLS DESIRE?

Our sexual desire is the place where our bodies and souls unite. Its desires are felt in both the material and immaterial parts of who we are. But though sexual desire is felt in the body, its command center is in our will, our person. We, not our bodies, are in control of our sexual desire. When we speak of controlling desire, we do not simply mean not acting upon one's desires but rather actually choosing that which one desires. But I fear many of us Christians have forgotten this fundamental truth. We readily affirm that a person can control his or her sexual activity, but we do not always affirm the idea that a person can control sexual desire.

Author Dannah Gresh, for example, though providing a great deal of helpful insight in the arena of sexual purity, mistakenly contends that sexual arousal is the result of a chemical reaction in the body and thus is uncontrollable. She states:

> Many of our bodies' responses are activated by the autonomic nervous system (ANS). This system is not controlled by the will, but

by the environment. Ever been in a fender-bender? Remember that sick feeling in your stomach and the rapid pulse? You felt physically different because of the environmental change. You cannot control these reactions by choice. The ANS forces the body to respond to the environment.

Sexual arousal works the same way. Things in the environment—what we see, what we hear, and what we smell—create sexual response. This is particularly strong in a man since God created him to be visually stimulated. If he sees a woman walk by wearing revealing clothing, what happens in his body? He may notice the change in his pulse, his body temperature will rise and blood begins to pump rapidly through his body. . . . While a man can choose how to respond to this arousal, he cannot control that it has occurred.[3]

We can speak from personal experience that such a view is simply not accurate. Though Gresh is correct about the biological factors of sexual arousal, she sources it incorrectly. Contrary to Gresh's conclusion, the autonomic nervous system (ANS) is not controlled by our environment but by our *perception* of the environment's effect on our well-being. The difference is significant. In a fender bender, it is not the accident itself that causes the ANS to respond, but, rather, our ANS responds to the *perception* that the pending accident could potentially threaten our well-being. When we perceive that the situation we are facing is dangerous, our bodies respond accordingly.

Let us consider an example. Suppose you are riding in a vehicle driven by a professional stunt driver. You hang on for dear life as the car careens around a twisty racetrack at speeds you never thought possible. As a first-time passenger, you are not convinced of the driver's ability to avoid a crash, thus your perception of the event as dangerous to your well-being causes your ANS to dump adrenaline into your system. Your pulse quickens, your breathing gets shorter, your stomach churns. But the stunt driver, on the other hand, has driven this particular track so many times he could do it in his sleep. Quite different from yours, his perception of the same environment has a far different effect on his ANS. His body does not respond with the same adrenaline rush, for he does not perceive the environment as threatening to his well-being.

If you were to safely ride with the stunt driver many more times on this same circuit, your ANS would respond quite differently from how it did the first time, for you would no longer perceive the ride as threatening to your well-being. Thus, again, it is not our environment (a wild car ride) that triggers our ANS but our *perception* of the environment's effect on our well-being.

Ultimately our ANS is triggered based upon the convictions we hold regarding all of life. It is because we firmly believe that guns, car wrecks, terminal illnesses, and growling dogs are all detrimental to our well-being that our ANS responds when we face those stimuli.

Our bodies respond automatically to our perception of not only negative environments but also to positive environments. This is seen in the body's response to sexual stimuli. But it is not the environment (scantily clad men or women, billboards, etc.) that triggers our ANS but rather our perception that the object is extremely beneficial to our well-being.

That sexual arousal is triggered by our perception of an object rather than by the object itself is seen in the decline of sexual desire when a sexual relationship has gone sour. Upon first sight of his mistress, a married man is extremely aroused. Wrongly, he perceives her as the absolute best thing for his well-being. Just the thought of her causes his pulse to quicken and his body to respond in sexual arousal. But as the relationship progresses, he finds she is not who he thought she was. Before long she is blackmailing him, threatening to make their relationship known unless he pays her off. Now suddenly the man no longer sees her as beneficial to his well-being. The very thought (let alone the sight) of her causes him to be sick to his stomach. He can't even imagine being sexually attracted to her. He hates her with a passion.

In this case, the same stimulus has two very different effects on the man based upon his perception of how it will affect his well-being. This transition from sexual desire to hatred is illustrated in the Bible as well. David's son Amnon followed an almost identical path when his sexual desire for his half sister Tamar turned into intense disgust (see 2 Sam. 13:1–17). So in the realm of sexual arousal, it is not the environment but our perception of the environment's benefit to our well-being that triggers our ANS.

SEXUAL SATISFACTION AND THE PEACE OF GOD

Augustine taught that our hearts are restless until they find rest in God alone. Our ANS is triggered so readily by the opposite sex, because nothing else in life so naturally seems to satiate the deep sense of restlessness that lurks within the human heart. As creatures that exist in the image of God, nothing comes closer to the genuine, all-satisfying experience of God than an intimate relationship with one who exists in that image. It is this same idea that caused one person to say that a man knocking on the door of a brothel is a man looking for God. Nothing comes closer to satisfying our restless need for spiritual union with God than the physical union of the sexual relationship.

When we fail to realize that true satisfaction can be found only in God, we often bounce from one sexual, romantic relationship to another, incorrectly assuming that the lack of satisfaction and sexual arousal we are feeling in the current relationship will be achieved in the next. Each new relationship, then, begins with the promise of ultimate satisfaction, and the ANS responds accordingly. But as the new relationship progresses, the promise of deep fulfillment is not met, and we no longer perceive it as beneficial for our well-being. Thus our ANS does not trigger sexual arousal with the same intensity. In each case the stimulus (the sexual relationship) does not change; what has changed is our perception of the relationship's ability to meet our deepest needs.[4]

BELIEVING THE TRUTH ABOUT SEXUAL IMMORALITY

When we are firmly convinced that sexual immorality is harmful to our well-being, it loses its grip on us and does not awaken within us sexual desire. Though we are fallen people for whom such conviction comes with great difficulty, it can indeed come. Such conviction takes great faith, but it grows as we embrace the unseen reality of Christ above and beyond what seems so immediately satisfying. We must by faith grasp firmly, and with deep conviction, the truths of God.

Do we really believe the path of the adulteress leads to death (Prov. 7:10, 27), that God will judge the sexually immoral who do not repent (Heb. 13:4; Rev. 21:8), and that no sexual satisfaction exists apart from living out the image of Christ's union to his bride? Our ANS will be the indicator.

Yet we will never become convinced of the truth of Christ until we are deeply united to the person of Christ. We must know Christ himself—his heart, his character—before we can have faith in his commands. We must not just *believe* that his ways are best; we must *know* that his ways are best. Such knowledge comes only through our personal experience with Christ himself. And such experience comes from our deep spiritual union with him via his Holy Spirit.

Ultimately, as we participate in the unseen reality of Christ, experiencing his very presence in our lives day to day, we grow in our convictions that his claims are in fact true, that his ways are indeed the best ways, and that nothing can satisfy apart from him.

Do we believe it is possible for a man to see a beautiful woman, perhaps dressed inappropriately, perhaps even attempting to seduce him, yet not desire her in his heart or be sexually aroused? Are we merely victims of our circumstances, needing to hide from the world lest we encounter anything that would force us to lust?

We must be firmly convinced that it is indeed possible to control and harness our desires, not merely our actions. To be sure, sexual desire is not controlled in the same manner we control our arms and legs; more than just a mere decision of the will is required. But we do control our sexual desire indirectly through what we believe about the reality of Christ, sexual immorality, and the truth of God. As we become absolutely convinced in our hearts and souls that God's ways are indeed the best ways, we will master our sexual desire.

Our bodies respond only in accordance with our convictions, and how we spontaneously react to life's circumstances will reveal what we believe. Just as it is possible to become a more spontaneously patient driver and a more instinctively gracious believer in Christ, so too it is possible to become more reflexively pure in our inadvertent encounters with the opposite sex. With the core belief that sexual desire is ultimately in our control, we *can* begin to build a life of inward purity.

CONCLUSION

It is important to understand what makes desire sinful. *Lust* (i.e., sinful desire) is "to desire something that is not ours to possess." This has significant application regarding both the sexual and romantic aspects of our sexuality. Anytime we desire something that is not ours to possess, we are sinning. In the next chapter we will see that God has instructed us to control our romantic desire until it can be properly expressed within the context of marriage.

Though you may be in full agreement up to this point, you might be wondering about the practicality of this perspective when it comes to finding a spouse. "Am I really not supposed to desire the opposite sex?" "How will I ever find a spouse?" Good questions! But rather than answering them now, let's save them for the next chapter.

DISCUSSION QUESTIONS

Read Matthew 5:27–28.

1) What makes some desires sinful and some pure?

2) How confident are you that you can control not only your sexual activity but also your sexual desire?

3) Think of a time in your life when your emotional, visceral response to an environment changed, even though the environment itself did not change. How does this relate to sexual arousal?

4) When is desire for a man or woman sinful?

5) When is desire for a man or woman not sinful?

6

FALLING IN LOVE ONCE

The Need to Guard Your Heart

Do not arouse or awaken love until it so desires.
THE BRIDE OF SOLOMON (SONG 2:7; 3:5 NIV)

In previous chapters we discussed God's standard for sexual purity (to the dismay of the men, no doubt). In this chapter we will explore God's wisdom for maintaining emotional and romantic integrity (to the dismay of the women, most likely). Ladies, if it seems like we're just a couple of grumpy old married men looking to wreck your next date with Mr. Right, give us an ear and wait until the next chapter. We have your best interest in mind, we assure you. Making wise choices about how and when to give away your heart—or how and when to win the heart of another—not only enables you to use your sexuality in a way that honors God but also provides you with the freedom and security that come from living out God's ideal.

As we will see, Scripture teaches that we are to guard our hearts, not awakening romantic love in ourselves or others until such love can seek legitimate fulfillment within the marriage relationship. There is a time to arouse romantic passions and a time to moderate them. Knowing the difference between the two is essential for making wise, godly choices about relationships. In this chapter we will discuss the appropriate occasions for moderating romantic passions, and in the next chapter we will discuss the appropriate context for bringing on the roses and the chocolate.

LESSONS FROM SOLOMON'S BRIDE

The Old Testament book Song of Solomon is a romantic diary of sorts, detailing the courtship between King Solomon and his bride. It is a clear statement about the beauty and worth of romantic love. In this short and sensual book, the two lovers unabashedly exalt the glory of their sexual, romantic relationship. Though much of the imagery in the book is foreign to the modern reader, we are immediately able to discern important truths about the appropriate timing and context for the release of romantic desire.

The opening verses of the second chapter are particularly helpful. Note the passionate language with which Solomon's bride describes her desire for her husband:

> Like an apple tree among the trees of the forest
>> is my lover among the young men.
> I delight to sit in his shade,
>> and his fruit is sweet to my taste.
> He has taken me to the banquet hall,
>> and his banner over me is love.
> Strengthen me with raisins,
>> refresh me with apples,
>> for I am faint with love.
> His left arm is under my head,
>> and his right arm embraces me.
> Daughters of Jerusalem, I charge you
>> by the gazelles and by the does of the field:
> Do not arouse or awaken love
>> until it so desires. (Song 2:3–7 NIV)[1]

The context of this passage focuses on the bride and the consummation of her relationship with Solomon. Apparently on the eve of her wedding, she describes herself as "faint with love" to the point that she needs to be refreshed with food. She is clearly swooning and delighting to do so. But note the charge Solomon's bride gives to the young maidens attending her: "Do not arouse or awaken love," she says, "until it so desires."

Fearing the arousal of her passions would likewise arouse the passions of the young women attending her, Solomon's bride exhorts the young women not to arouse or awaken their sexual, romantic passions until "love so desires." The phrase is arresting. Solomon's bride is not simply saying, "Don't arouse or awaken love until *you* desire." No. The release from this charge is when love, not the person, desires. Love is personified in this passage as the guardian and keeper of itself. It doesn't want to be awakened prior to the occasion for which it was created. In the case of Solomon's bride, love has obviously granted permission to be awakened, for the bride has approached a place in life in which sexual, romantic love can be rightly consummated. The maidens, however, are not in a life circumstance where nuptials are pending. Consequently, they are told to refrain from arousing romantic love. The implications are clear: romantic love is to be aroused within the context of a marriage relationship (or pending marriage relationship).

It's worth making the observation that we are nowhere here instructed to suppress or deny our God-given desires for sex and romance. Rather, we are told to refrain from stirring up such passions. The picture is much like that of a fire that has been allowed to burn down to a bed of hot coals. Within the coals is the potential for a raging fire, given the proper stirring up. When it comes to premarital sexual, romantic desires, this is precisely what we are not supposed to do.

And of course this makes a good deal of sense when we consider again the tenuous nature of pre-engagement relationships. As we observed in chapter 4, there can be no true commitment apart from a marriage proposal. Thus, the arousal of our sexual, romantic passions within a relationship that has no declared intention of moving toward marriage is misguided. It's like spending every weekend at the car dealership when you have no money. And you're twelve. The point is pretty simple: don't get yourself romantically and sexually charged up about a relationship that isn't explicitly moving toward a wedding. Not only is it emotionally foolish; it's morally irresponsible.

A WRONG FIXATION ON RIGHT DESIRES

In every area of life, there is a need to regulate our desires. Fantasies and daydreams can get us into trouble. The man who fixates on material possessions he can't afford sets himself up for dissatisfaction and/or a maxed-out credit card. The overweight woman who desires to lose weight but spends her days watching the cooking channel isn't making her life any easier. The enjoyment of food and material possessions is fine, as far as it goes. But too much of a good thing, or a good thing at the wrong time, becomes a bad thing. The same holds true for our romantic passions. Romantic desire was designed by God to propel us toward sexual desire, and sexual desire was designed to propel us toward sexual activity. An inordinate fixation on romantic desire disconnected from the context in which such desires can be properly expressed will, more often than not, lead to foolish choices. The man who intends chastity but romances every girl he dates is at cross purposes with himself.

Romantic attention is, at its core, an invitation to move into a deeper level of intimacy. And there can be no denying that romantic attention—by its very nature—seeks sexual intimacy. Maybe you haven't ever thought about it like that, but it's true. When a man romances a woman, he is attempting to gain access to that certain part of her that she reserves exclusively for her lover. When he brings her flowers and chocolates and jewelry and tells her how pretty she is, he isn't looking to be just friends. The natural (and appropriate) end of romance is the bedroom.

Now, we've no problem with a man romancing a woman with a view to sexual intimacy (as you'll see in the next chapter). But we do have a problem with a man romancing a woman outside of the context in which sexual intimacy can be properly expressed. Our sexual passions are hard enough to control without fanning them into flame. Why make life harder on ourselves than it needs to be? Romance is a wonderful thing when set within the marital context. But when disconnected from the trajectory of marriage, an over-preoccupation with romance has a tendency to propel us down roads that we are not yet ready to travel.

This truth has obvious implications for how we do pre-engagement relationships. We'll pick this up in detail in the next chapter, but it hardly bears observing that contemporary dating relationships aren't helping us guard our hearts. Most dating relationships are—if nothing else—an explicit occasion for romantic intimacy. This preoccupation with romance pushes the relationship in a subtly (and often not-so-subtly) sexual direction. The net effect is all too often deep emotional pain for both the man and the woman.

BRUISED BUT NOT BROKEN

Unrequited love may be an inevitable part of life, but a bruised heart is better than a broken heart. Dating relationships become inappropriate when they serve as a context for a man and a woman to intentionally stir up romantic and sexual intimacy in the other. On what grounds does a man or woman have the right to stir up passions in another that he or she cannot legitimately satisfy? So many dating relationships are little more than a romantic entanglement in which a man invites a woman to give him her heart (and often her body), while all the while he has made no real commitment to her and has no real idea about his long term plans for the relationship.

Of course we're realists here. We were young and in love once too. The point is not that one should try to repress his or her romantic feelings or that being attracted toward a member of the opposite sex is wrong. The charge given by Solomon's bride is that we avoid intentionally doing things that are explicitly designed to arouse and awaken sexual desire outside the marriage relationship. It's natural to feel attracted to a person you are viewing as a potential mate. Well and good. You should. But feeling an attraction and fanning into flame that attraction are two different things.

Jackie and Mike have been getting to know each other in earnest over the past four months. Jackie is divorced (her husband had an affair and left her, despite her attempts at reconciliation) and Mike has a "before Christ" past checkered with poor choices when it comes to relationships. Both have grown a lot in the last few years, and both are interested in marriage. But Jackie and Mike are taking it slow. More than anything they want to find out what really matters most about the other—character, priorities in life, love for the Lord. These are the sorts of things that make a marriage last. Mike doesn't bring Jackie roses. He doesn't take her out to expensive dinners. He doesn't buy her jewelry or compliment her looks in a sexually nuanced way. He doesn't hold her hand and stare into her eyes and tell her how beautiful she is. They are a couple of friends getting to know each other. Of course, it's a special sort of friendship: they both know marriage is a possibility. But Mike hasn't made up his mind about whether Jackie is the one, and Jackie hasn't made up her mind about Mike, so neither one is getting out ahead of the relationship.

Only God knows what the future holds for Mike and Jackie. And no doubt if one of them redirects the friendship away from marriage, to the disappointment of the other, certainly there will be some emotional pain. But the pain will be substantially less than it otherwise might have been in a contemporary dating relationship. As Jackie said, "No matter what happens, we haven't done anything we regret. If he marries someone else, I'll be able to look Mike and his wife in the eye without shame."

Contrary to popular opinion, broken hearts need not be a standard part of premarital relationships. To be sure, no relationship can ever be entirely safe from heartache. But it is certainly less painful to disengage emotionally from a relationship that has remained essentially platonic than from a relationship that has been deeply romantic.

CONCLUSION

The need for romantic responsibility relates back to the image of Christ and the church. To romantically woo a woman, or to give your heart away to a man, prior to a marriage commitment is to paint an unclear portrait of Christ and the church. From the beginning of time, Christ has reserved his deepest affections and desires for the church, even before he met her. And from the earliest days of creation, the saints have waited with monogamous longing for the coming of the Promised One. This image must be expressed within our own wait for marriage. Christ was faithful in body and heart to a bride whom he had not yet met. He reserved his deepest affection for the one whom God had given him, and, likewise, we are called to the same faithfulness.

Ultimately then, we are not to stir up sexual, romantic love in our hearts (or the heart of another) outside the context of a marriage relationship. We must refrain from doing things—whether relationally or otherwise—that cause us to arouse romantic love in our hearts prior to our ability to properly consummate such love in a marriage relationship.

But, you ask, is it ever right to stoke the coals of romance and passion? Indeed it is. And that's what the next chapter is about.

DISCUSSION QUESTIONS

1) According to Song of Solomon 2:3–7, when is the proper time to arouse and awaken our desire for someone?

2) What are ways that we might inappropriately arouse or awaken love?

3) Why does God command us to refrain from arousing our romantic and sexual passions until we are married?

7

DATING FRIENDSHIPS

Switching Categories without Creating New Ones

For this is the will of God, your sanctification:
that you abstain from sexual immorality.
THE APOSTLE PAUL (1 THESS. 4:3)

Jennifer reached across the table and closed Tom's menu. "They come more quickly when they know you're done looking at the menu," she said.

Tom laughed. "Who are you, so wise in the ways of ordering?"

Jennifer smiled. "I have many secrets."

"Speaking of secrets . . . " Tom paused and looked down. He folded his napkin in half and then unfolded it again. "I was hoping to get to know some of them," he said, looking up.

Jennifer's look was not discouraging, but neither was it inviting. He took a breath.

Tom was the junior-high pastor at their church, and Jennifer volunteered with the high-school group. The two groups met on the same night, so Tom and Jennifer often saw each other but usually just in passing. They had gotten to know one another a bit during the staff meetings and weekend leadership retreats held each year for the junior- and senior-high workers. They had never really had a lot of time to get to know each other on a personal level, but more and more Tom found himself noticing her comings and goings. After praying about his growing attraction toward her, he finally decided it was time to see where all of this might lead.

Jennifer looked across the room and then back at Tom. Her face was kind but also apologetic. "I don't in any way want to be presumptuous, but I just want to be upfront with you. I got out of a pretty rough relationship six months ago. I'm not sure I'm interested in any kind of relationship right now. I just don't want you wasting your time and energy. It wouldn't be fair."

Tom smiled and leaned back in his chair. He put his hands up as if to signal her to slow down. "I totally understand. I should have explained what I meant. I'm not interested in a relationship either, if what you mean by *relationship* is what most people mean. It's just that I don't know you that well and we don't have many opportunities to get to know each other, so I thought it might be nice to spend some time getting to know each other. I'm not looking for a girlfriend."

Jennifer gave Tom a puzzled look. "You want to get to know me, but you're not looking for a girlfriend. I don't think I'm following you."

Tom nodded in understanding. "Well, to be really frank, I'm not looking for a girlfriend; I'm looking for a wife. And," he quickly added, feeling his face flush, "I don't mean to say that that's you for sure." He shrugged his shoulder. "Who knows? But that's why I want to get to know you. Look, it's like this: doing the whole boyfriend-girlfriend thing seems kind of pointless. I mean, where does that really get you anyway? It's just two people agreeing to like each other until they don't feel like liking each other anymore. There's no real commitment, and people end up giving their hearts away, and then the whole thing falls apart. I'd rather just date and stay friends with a girl right up until engagement, since that's the only real commitment two people can make toward one another anyway. That way, if things don't pan out, no one gets as hurt. And if the relationship *does* lead to marriage, you haven't lost anything.

So I don't plan on asking you—or anyone for that matter—for any kind of commitment. I just want to get to know you better."

Jennifer was quiet for a moment and then finally said, "I can't decide if that's less pressure or more. It sounds like you're not asking me to enter into any kind of formal relationship at all, which to be honest sounds nice right now. But at the same time you're wanting to get to know me to see if you want me for a wife."

Tom smiled sheepishly. "Yeah, I know it's a bit unconventional. Think of it like a 'dating friendship,' instead of a traditional dating relationship; friends who go out on dates and get to know each other, but who don't attempt to be anything more than friends until they're sure they know what they want."

Jennifer gave Tom a quizzical look. "What happens when you finally decide what you want? Do you do the boyfriend-girlfriend thing then?"

"No. If I came to the conclusion that I wanted to marry a girl— and that's what I mean by 'knowing what I want'—then I would ask her to marry me, not ask her to be my girlfriend. Like I said before, I don't have much use for the whole dating relationship thing. I'd just move straight from friendship to engagement—that's if *she* wanted to as well, of course," he added with a smile.

Jennifer didn't say anything, so Tom continued. "Really there's no pressure at all. I just want to become better friends. Go out a few times; get to know each other. If at some point you know for sure that there could never be anything more than a friendship, just tell me, and that's all there will ever be. And I'll do the same for you. In the meantime, feel free to date whom you want, do what you want, whatever. I don't want any more right to dictate what you do with your life than I had yesterday. Let's just be friends and see what happens."

After a long pause Jennifer spoke. "I think I like the sound of this. And especially since coming out of my last relationship, the whole thing is beginning to make a lot of sense. But I'm not sure I totally get it yet. And since we're going to be friends, the first thing I'd like from you is to keep explaining how these 'dating friendships' work. It may come in handy someday."

DATING FRIENDSHIPS: THE ALTERNATIVE TO DATING RELATIONSHIPS

So how does one go about finding a spouse if not by the typical means of a dating relationship? What we propose in this chapter is neither complex nor particularly innovative. But its simplicity, we believe, is its greatest strength. We propose that a man and a woman considering marriage establish a dating friendship. Our idea of a dating friendship is pretty straightforward. We define a dating friendship as "two friends getting to know each other with a view toward marriage." That's it. Not very complicated, is it?

Think of a dating friendship as a precursor to a marriage proposal but without all the romantic, sexual overtones that so often accompany a typical dating relationship. A couple in a dating friendship, regardless of their attraction toward each other, doesn't pretend there is more to the relationship than is warranted. They consciously refrain from sexual and overtly romantic activity and don't become naively optimistic about the commitment level of their friendship. Thus, the main goal of a dating friendship is to explore the viability of marriage while preserving the guidelines of sexual and romantic purity required by the neighbor relationship (see chapter 1).

So what happens when a dating friendship has run its course? Once a dating friendship has established clarity regarding the relationship, a couple will either disengage and return to a "normal" friendship, or the man—convinced that he wants to marry the woman—will ask her to marry him. If she remains uncertain, he will use everything in his romantic arsenal to convince her that he's the one. (More on that in a moment.)

DISTINCTIVES OF A DATING FRIENDSHIP

Though we believe Scripture allows for a great deal of flexibility when it comes to pre-engagement relationships, four elements are crucial to any couple exploring the possibility of marriage: (1) maintaining the guidelines of sexual and romantic purity found in the neighbor relationship; (2) communicating clearly about one's intentions; (3) viewing dating as an activity rather than a category of relationship; and (4) considering a relationship's exclusivity as voluntary. A dating friendship is specifically designed to incorporate all four of these elements. Let's look at each in turn.

Maintaining the Boundaries of the Neighbor Relationship

Perhaps most significantly, a dating friendship is committed to upholding the sexual purity guidelines of the neighbor relationship. Both parties have an agreement that they will not cross these boundaries and that the requirements of purity for their relationship are no different from any other relationship. Too many of our current dating practices do not take seriously the scriptural mandates for sexual and romantic purity found in 1 Corinthians 7:1–9 and Song of Solomon 2:1–7. A dating friendship does.

Of course, careful thought must be given as to the moral guardrails that will help protect a dating friendship from dissolving into a sexual relationship. The commitment not to light oneself on fire—while good as far as it goes—will not get one very far if one chooses to douse oneself in gasoline and play with matches. What follows are a few suggestions about how a couple might structure its relationship in a way that makes purity an achievable goal.

Get accountability. Godly accountability will play a large role in maintaining the purity of a dating friendship. Sin thrives in isolation, and having someone who cares about you—and whom you respect—checking up on you and praying for you will go a long way toward making sure the dating friendship stays on course. We encourage both the man and the woman to have separate account-ability partners. Accountability partners should be people who are godly and wise, who understand the Bible's perspective on purity (give them a copy of this book!), and who aren't afraid to poke into your life with pointed questions. Seeking out godly, grace-filled accountability places you in submission to the Christian community and allows godly Christians to evaluate your dating friendship in light of the gospel.

Avoid alone time. In Romans 13:14 we are instructed to "make no provision for the flesh." As you are no doubt aware, your flesh doesn't need much help when it comes to sinful behavior. Which is exactly the reason why a dating friendship should avoid dating con-texts that push it toward intimacy. Avoid spending time alone at each other's apartment. Don't hang out alone in a car. Keep the lights on. As much as possible, keep your relationship in public view. And be forward thinking in how you spend your time together. What may be easy for you to do early in the relationship (spending time alone in her apartment) will become increasingly difficult as the relationship progresses. Establish healthy patterns of relating early in the friend-ship. Believe us when we say that you will not regret being cautious.

Be outward facing. A sign of a healthy relationship is that it isn't always turned inward. Of course, it is appropriate for a dating friendship to have an inward focus some of the time; you are, after all, getting to know each other with a view toward marriage. But avoid having *only*—or even *primarily*—an inward focus. A healthy relationship looks beyond itself and engages the world around it. A healthy relationship is comfortable being in community. This out-ward facing posture will help you cultivate a missional edge, which is important for a healthy marriage. Your marriage, one day, should be used for others. Start to live that way from the start.

Begin at the right time. Start a dating friendship only when you know you are in a position (or soon to be in a position) to get mar-ried. Too many singles begin too early and thus put themselves in a precarious situation. For instance, a lot of college students start dating at the beginning of college, with little thought about where the relationship might lead. Not long into their dating relationship they come to realize they want to marry the person they are dating. That's the good news. The bad news is that they are not at a place in life where marriage is a realistic possibility. So there they are, one foot on the brake and the other on the gas, with years to go. Love has been awakened before it desired, stressing out their heart and bodies in ways not intended by God.

Of course, in our modern dating culture this tension is alleviated through premature sexual activity. Couples are able to date for years precisely because they are already dipping into sexual activity; dinner can wait, because the appetizers are being served. One can easily see why our current dating culture is ambivalent toward long-term dating relationships. Couples get the benefits of marriage while avoiding the responsibilities. But a dating friendship aims for something higher than a traditional dating relationship.

Yet even in a dating friendship—where sexual and romantic activity has been intentionally avoided—the emotional and sexual pull can become problematic if the relationship lasts too long. So, we recommend that you hold off on initiating a dating friendship until you are at a place in life where marriage is a realistic possibility. We can't think of any good reason why the typical high school student would begin a dating friendship, let alone a dating relationship. Be friends. Hang out in groups. Have a great time! But trust God's plan for relationships and wait until you are ready for marriage before you begin to look for a spouse.

Keep it short. Following on the last point, once you begin a dating friendship, do not tarry longer than necessary. How long is too long? It varies from person to person, but assuming you're both at a place in life where it is appropriate to marry, six to eighteen months seems about right. Wait any longer, and purity becomes increasingly more challenging. Get to know the other person, pray about the friendship, seek godly counsel, and then make a decision. If you're still uncertain after eighteen months, that's probably an indication something is wrong in the relationship.

Make a beeline to the altar. And one last word about timing: if things work out and you get engaged, keep your engagement short. Engagement exists for one purpose only—to plan a wedding. It is not a final vetting process or an attempt to buy time while your parents warm to the idea. Too many Christian couples are sacrificing their purity on the altar of a perfect wedding day. So don't think of engagement as über-dating, where you buy more time and have the benefit of a closed deal. Engagement is there to plan a wedding. Once she says yes, it's beeline time.

Clear Communication

A second crucial element of a dating friendship, given its uniqueness, is clear and forthright communication between both parties. Likely one of the parties will not understand the concept of a dating friendship, so it will be important to communicate one's purpose and intent from the outset (as done in our opening vignette). For example, a woman who is operating under the traditional mind-set of dating would likely become confused by the actions of a man who had not communicated his commitment to the format of a dating friendship.

In keeping with the image of Christ's pursuit of the church, it would seem to be the man's responsibility to declare his interest in the woman as a potential marriage partner. If she knows for sure that she has no interest in ever moving beyond the neighbor relationship, she can let him know immediately.

But, ladies, what do you do if he's not making his intentions known? It is well within a woman's right to inquire about a man's intentions. At some point a man owes a woman an explanation regarding his advances. Is he looking for a hang-out friend? Is he getting to know her with a view to marriage? Is he just looking for a traditional dating relationship, with marriage a far distant objective? In any event, a woman is wise to seek clarification early on in a relationship. Without such information she is unable to gauge the wisdom of investing in the relationship.

Dating as an Activity Rather Than a Category of Relationship

We've already discussed the distinction between dating as an activity and as a category of relationship, so we need not belabor it here. Suffice it to say, however, that two people looking at each other as potential marriage partners do not, on the basis of their mutual attraction, have any grounds for establishing a category of relationship distinct from the neighbor relationship. Thus, a couple in a dating friendship will view dating as an activity rather than as a category of relationship. In other words, dating is something they *do* rather than something they *are*. This distinction between dating as an activity and as a category helps to maintain the truth that all unmarried men and women must relate under the purity guidelines established in the neighbor relationship.

Dating Friendships and Voluntary Exclusivity

Since no new category of relationship has been established, the exclusivity of the relationship can be only voluntary (self-imposed) rather than seemingly mandated by the relationship itself. True exclusivity is not possible apart from marriage or engagement. To think otherwise is a recipe for heartache.

This does not mean that a man and a woman cannot *voluntarily* choose to limit their interaction with the opposite sex. Not only is this permissible, but also we recommend it. For example, if a young man is particularly interested in a specific woman, he will likely not want to spend time and energy developing significant relationships with other women.

A woman, likewise, may choose to turn down dates from other men when she knows that her interests lie elsewhere. But again, it is important to remember that there can be no real promise of exclusivity apart from marriage or engagement. So in a dating friendship each person is free to choose to be exclusive throughout the duration of the relationship. The relationship itself cannot demand it. It may even be the case that a man will limit his dating activities to a particular woman, but she may choose not to be exclusive in return (or vice versa). More about the idea of voluntary exclusivity will be addressed in the "Objections" section below.

This lack of forced exclusivity goes a long way toward shattering the façade of commitment in pre-engagement relationships. As we argued extensively in chapter 6, there can be no real commitment apart from a marriage proposal. Thus it seems wise to us that a man and woman avoid using terms such as *promise* and *commitment*. Refusing to use such words in a pre-engagement relationship helps to maintain a proper perspective on the true nature of the relationship. Until a marriage proposal is offered and accepted, there can be no real commitment between an unmarried man and woman.

ADVANTAGES OF DATING FRIENDSHIPS

A dating friendship has many advantages over a traditional dating relationship, the first being its capacity to clarify the bounds of the neighbor relationship. This helps to protect individuals from the hurt that can come from premature romantic and sexual expression. It also allows two people to get to know each other without the distractions of a physical and romantic relationship, which in many ways can mask the true qualities of the relationship. Further, a dating friendship is entirely consistent with Scripture. Finally, and most importantly, a dating friendship helps to preserve the image of God that he intends our sexuality to portray. We will look at each of these advantages in turn.

The Neighbor Relationship Preserved

The major advantage of a dating friendship is that it in no way blurs the boundaries of the neighbor relationship. Because no new category of relationship is created or assumed, the nonsexual aspect of the neighbor relationship is more clearly recognized and thus preserved. Even apart from biblical revelation, most Christians (and even some non-Christians) have a sense that the expression of romantic and sexual affection is out of bounds within the neighbor relationship. Understanding that two people are called to remain within the neighbor relationship until marriage is fundamental to a life of romantic and sexual purity. Remaining friends until engagement keeps this boundary clearly before the man and the woman.

Free from Distractions

There is nothing a person can discover in a dating relationship or courtship that cannot equally be discovered through a dating friendship. Life dreams, priorities, values, backgrounds, and character qualities can all be gleaned through a friendship. One does not need to establish a separate category of relationship to discern these things. In fact, we would argue that these important character qualities and life goals can be even more readily discerned within the context of a dating friendship.

Many dating relationships are based almost solely upon the romantic and sexual attraction that exists between the couple. But strip this away and they will discover that they have almost nothing in common and really nothing to talk about. If a couple cannot develop a friendship apart from a sexually-tinged dating relationship, then marriage would be an ill-advised next step. But a friendship that is free from the distractions of a sexual, romantic relationship has the opportunity to stand or fall on its own merit rather than being merely propped up by ebbing passion and desires.

Freer from Heartache

Though no relationship can be totally free of heartache, a dating friendship helps make heartache less likely. A friend of ours was introduced to a woman through a mutual friend, and the two of them initially hit it off. Committed to the basic principles of a dating friendship, he expressed to us the unusual feeling he had as the relationship progressed. Used to jumping in with both feet, he found it both relaxing and comfortable getting to know a woman without the distractions of romance and a physical relationship. And after dating casually for a number of months, it became apparent to both of them that neither desired to move beyond the neighbor relationship.

They have instead remained friends, seeing each other on occasion without the regret that would have come from an aborted intimate, romantic relationship. He later confided to us that had the two of them become romantically and physically involved (as had happened in his prior relationships), it would have taken much longer to discern that there was no future in the relationship and it would have ended painfully for one or both of them.

This is not to say that feelings of disappointment can be eliminated entirely. Heartache may indeed arise for one party if the friendship never results in marriage. Disappointment and sorrow are legitimate feelings that should accompany the loss of any good thing. But all things being equal, the pain of loss within a dating friendship is considerably less than the pain that comes from traditional dating relationships, since a dating friendship consciously maintains both physical and romantic purity.

Consistent with Scripture

Not insignificantly, a dating friendship fits well with the Bible's silence regarding finding a spouse. If God had wanted us to develop an official system by which we moved from one category of relationship to another, it seems likely that he would have informed us of it. Perhaps we should interpret his silence as an indication that he did not desire us to develop such a system.

Since the Bible does not prescribe a middle stage between the neighbor relationship and the marriage relationship, we should be slow in doing so as well. Maintaining a friendship with a prospective spouse until engagement in no way impedes the future marriage and fits readily with the biblical expectations that God places upon men and women in the neighbor relationship.

Protecting God's Image

Most significantly, a dating friendship helps to preserve the image of God that human sexuality is meant to express. When we understand that, by entering into a dating friendship, no categories of relationship have been switched, the temptation to become romantically dependent and sexually involved is lessened. No shadow relationship of dating exists in which one can fall under the false assumption that it is safe and proper to begin giving him- or herself away. And this, of course, finds its ultimate meaning in the truth of Christ's single-minded devotion and affection for the church. Christ waited faithfully for his bride, and thus we must wait for ours in a similar fashion. Christ fell in love once; we fall in love once.

The image of God that resides within our sexuality is of great value, and our desire to protect it is greatly serviced by refusing to create categories of relationships that appear to be distinct from the neighbor relationship and thus seemingly free from its commands of sexual purity.

OBJECTIONS TO DATING FRIENDSHIPS

In communicating this approach, we have encountered a variety of objections. Though by no means exhaustive, the following objections typify the general concerns that some singles have with our idea of a dating friendship.

Objection 1: A dating friendship is too vulnerable, since it lacks commitment.

A young woman expressed her concern with dating friendships by saying, "Looking for a spouse requires you to open up and become vulnerable. I'm not going to bare my soul with some guy who hasn't made any commitment to me and might be dating other women."

We would agree wholeheartedly with her concern. A woman would indeed be unwise to become vulnerable to a guy who was not sure what he wanted. Any man who is serious about a particular woman will limit his interaction with other women. But the woman he is interested in must remember that regardless of whether he is her boyfriend, any exclusivity is only self-imposed. To think otherwise is a breach of sound judgment. It does her little good to desire the security that comes from an apparently exclusive relationship when, in fact, such security does not really exist.

Singles must enter into relationships with their eyes open, fully aware that man-made titles such as "boyfriend" and "girlfriend" in no way provide any real measure of security. The fact that two people openly acknowledge their attraction toward one another does not guarantee that such attraction will be permanent.

It is true that a dating friendship offers no security, but its main advantage is that, unlike traditional dating relationships, it doesn't *pretend* to. In our estimation, this makes it a much safer method. By not requiring exclusivity, the risks of finding a spouse are fully exposed. In a traditional dating relationship, the man or woman is able to walk away at any time. Doing so would in no way break any commitment. The man has not promised to marry the woman, and she has no right to expect that he will.

For a woman to feel that a traditional dating relationship offers a context in which it is safe to become vulnerable is a feeling based on falsehood. Nothing is inherently more secure in a traditional dating or courting relationship than in a dating friendship. The more we are aware of this, the more accurately we can make informed decisions about whom we will choose to become vulnerable with—and the more carefully we will guard our hearts.

Indeed, we would argue that the self-imposed exclusivity of a dating friendship is grounds for greater security than that of a traditional dating relationship. In a dating friendship, a man chooses to limit his interaction with the opposite sex because he wants to. When a woman sees this exclusivity, she knows that it is sincere, freely chosen, and from the heart. In contrast, how is it more secure for a woman to believe the reason her boyfriend dates her exclusively is that the relationship requires it of him? When the exclusivity is recognized as voluntary, the woman is fully aware of a man's attraction toward her, as well as his present unwillingness to make a permanent commitment. From this perspective, she now has the ability to make wise choices about how vulnerable she will choose to be with him.

Objection 2: A dating friendship is unable to give enough information regarding the appropriateness of a future marriage.

"How am I supposed to know if I want to get engaged to a particular person," one might argue, "if I do not develop a dating relationship first?" But how does establishing a pseudo commitment and actively engaging in sexual activity really help a man and woman discover whether they will be a good husband or wife?

Expressing one's sexual, romantic passion does not provide any useful information in determining the viability of a potential spouse; rather, it can cloud one's ability to think wisely about the issue. Everything a person needs to know about another can be learned in a dating friendship. One does not need to give or receive sexual expression to know whether they want to do so. The idea that a traditional dating relationship must be established in order to really know a person is false.

Objection 3: It's not reasonable to think that we can treat a person we are considering for marriage as "just a friend."

Some singles we have spoken with about dating friendships often initially find it difficult to think of a person they are considering marrying as "just a friend." And indeed, two people in a dating friendship are not just friends. As one single man once stated, "When I ask a girl out on a date, the fact of the matter is that I'm looking for something different from her than I am from my other friends that are women."

We would not at all contest this observation. Clearly there are many sub-relationships within the broad category of the neighbor relationship. Many of these relationships have very different agendas, purposes, and levels of emotional attachment. Business relationships, good friends, best friends, mere acquaintances, future spouses, and even pastoral relationships all necessitate different types of interaction, intimacy, and emotional involvement. Yet they all fall within the larger category of the neighbor relationship.

The neighbor relationship does not insist that all relationships within it are the same, but only that the guidelines of romantic and sexual purity are the same for each relationship. For example, though the interaction between a pastor and congregant and a prospective husband and wife will entail different kinds of interaction, both relationships are called to keep their interaction within the guidelines of purity established by the neighbor relationship.

Thus, the aim of a dating friendship is not to pretend that distinctions within the neighbor relationship (and hopes for marriage) do not exist, but rather to help both parties keep a clear perspective on what such a relationship does and does not entail. It *does* entail two people looking for a spouse. It does *not* entail two people who have already found one.

Objection 4: A dating friendship isn't practical in today's society.

Since when do we determine truth based on practicality? Though the least spoken, this is perhaps the foundational objection leveled by many detractors of dating friendships. Often when speaking to singles, we encounter no resistance as to the content of what we are saying, yet we still encounter resistance regarding our conclusions. It is as though they agree with us, and even agree that the Bible seems to teach what we are suggesting, but the thought of actually trying to live out this ideal within our contemporary society seems so impossible as to be beyond reach.

Jesus encountered this same situation when he taught on divorce. When his disciples were told that divorce was permissible only for marital unfaithfulness, they were astounded and exclaimed, "If such is the case of a man with his wife, it is better not to marry" (Matt. 19:10). In Jesus's day, divorce laws were so lax that a man could divorce his wife for almost any reason. Jesus's teaching was so restrictive, given the social context of his day, that his command seemed almost to negate the whole idea of marriage. But the disciples' dismay arose from their lack of faith in the possibility of keeping Christ's commands.

Some may not agree that the Bible teaches what we are suggesting. If you find yourself among them, then you have the freedom of conscience to follow a different path. But those of us who have become convinced otherwise are bound by what we believe the Bible to teach. We cannot simply declare Scripture unpractical and then set it aside for something more expedient.

WHEN TO TURN IT ON

At some point a dating friendship will do its job. A man and woman will have clarity about the wisdom of moving forward into marriage. As we noted earlier, it is irresponsible for a man to try to win a woman's heart before he knows what he plans to do with it. And it's irresponsible for a woman to give her heart away to a man who has not pledged to keep it. Everything changes, however, once clarity regarding marriage has been achieved. Once a man has determined he desires a particular woman for a wife (not simply as a girlfriend!), then we wish him Godspeed in wooing her. It might be that she will acquiesce at once to his offer of marriage. But it could be that she will need more time. Either way is fine.

If he's certain and she isn't, it's time for him to adopt a new posture in the relationship. When the dating friendship started, neither party was certain about the long-term viability of the relationship. But now that the man knows for certain that he wants to marry the woman, he should spare no expense in securing her affection. He should buy her flowers, tell her how beautiful her hair looks in the light, take her out to a fancy dinner, and, most importantly, *buy her a ring*. In short, the time to bring on the romance is when you're ready to bring on the ring!

The bold (yet appropriately sensitive) pursuit of a bride fits neatly with the image of Christ and the church. In a very real sense, Christ spared no expense in winning our affection. He laid it on the line. And he made it clear at the outset that he wasn't playing around. A would-be groom does well to follow the lead of the master suitor. Thus it is appropriate for a man to seek to arouse a woman's romantic affections precisely because he intends—if she will consent—to satisfy those affections within the context of marriage.

But men, listen up (and women, listen in). When it comes to winning the affections of a woman, please bear in mind three important things. First, you are trying to win her as your *wife*, not as your girlfriend. She should know at the outset that you are playing for keeps. And the clearest way for her to know—really the *only* way for her to know—is for you to propose. This completely changes the dynamics of the relationship and sets the whole thing on a collision course with marriage. Once a marriage proposal has been offered, it is no longer irresponsible for you to attempt to woo her heart, and no longer is it irresponsible for her to give it away.

Second, your attempt to woo a woman's heart must be done with respect to the sexual purity guidelines of the neighbor relationship. The fact that you desire to marry a woman does not mean that you have yet married her. As such, you do not have the right to access her sexuality, even in minor ways. She may ultimately say no to your marriage proposal, in which case you are responsible for ensuring her sexual integrity for whomever she does end up marrying. Don't take what isn't properly yours. The brother-sister test is still the litmus test for purity.

And finally, part of your job is to help the woman you are pursuing make a good decision about your marriage proposal. Don't assume your judgment is the only judgment that counts. In the midst of pouring on the romance, don't pour it on so thick that she is unable to see the reality for the roses. She may need some space to think soberly, carefully, and prayerfully about what God wants for her (and you). Ultimately you want her to say yes because she has peace before the Lord and not simply because you told her how pretty she looked in the moonlight. (Women, we know most of you are too smart for the "your hair looks pretty" line. We're just trying to help the men gain a proper sense of responsibility.)

This way of doing things, of course, puts the man in a position of vulnerability. He's making an offer of marriage with no guarantee that she'll say yes. But that's how it should be. Guys, it's time to man up when it comes to marriage proposals. Don't make her say yes before you've asked her. This puts the woman in the position of vulnerability. She's laid her cards on the table, and yours are still pressed against the vest. In keeping with the image of Christ's pursuit of the church, the man must be willing to be the first to declare his affections, bearing the weight of vulnerability in the relationship.

CONCLUSION

Well, there you have it. If the picture of a dating friendship does not seem like it entails much romance or security, keep in mind that experiencing romance and security is not its objective. Its only objective is to determine the viability of marriage. All the romance, passion, intimacy, and security that you long for is waiting for you in marriage. Traditional dating relationships, though they may appear to provide these things, are really only shadow relationships that offer nothing concrete. Since no promise can be made apart from engagement, it is wise to establish relationships based on this reality.

A dating friendship protects sexuality and allows the fruit to ripen on the vine so it can be enjoyed to its fullest capacity within the context of marriage. It is not slowly nibbled away in relationship after relationship, rendering unclear the single-minded nature of Christ's relationship with the church.

Regardless of what method you use to pursue a spouse, keep in mind the fundamental guidelines of the neighbor relationship. Any system that appears to remove two people from the confines of this relationship is misguided and creates potential for great harm to both yourself and the image of God.

DISCUSSION QUESTIONS

1) How would you explain dating friendships to a friend? What is the main goal?

2) What are the four crucial elements in any male-female relationship in which the couple is exploring the possibility of marriage?

3) What advantages do dating friendships have over traditional dating relationships?

4) How would you answer someone who argues that a dating friendship offers a couple no security?

8

AN INTEGRATED LIFE

Purity as a Lifestyle, Not Just as a Dating Thing

"All things are lawful for me," but not all things are helpful.
"All things are lawful for me," but I will not
be enslaved by anything.
THE APOSTLE PAUL (1 COR. 6:12)

It would be far easier to limit our discussion of purity to the topic of dating. While the purpose of our book has been this narrower field, this chapter addresses the subject of sexual purity more broadly. But first, a quick recap of where we've been.

In the beginning chapters we articulated a biblical theology of sex that sought to connect human sexuality with the spiritual relationship between Christ and the church. Sexuality, we argued, has been ordained by God as a means of reflecting the gospel and therefore must be expressed in keeping with the logic, rhythms, and function of the gospel. Christ is spiritually faithful to the church; the husband must be sexually faithful to his wife. Christ makes himself spiritually one with the church alone; a man makes himself sexually one with his wife alone. Christ has one bride; a man has one wife. The heavenly reality serves as the pattern for earthly practice.

In fact, as one studies Scripture, it should not surprise us that the gospel informs not only our understanding of sexuality and human relationships but also all of life. God has created the world to be a reflection—a living theater, if you will—of the gospel. Thus, every facet of human life is organically connected via the gospel. Just as our head is connected to our feet by our nervous system, so too our sexuality is connected to every other part of life through mutual participation in the gospel. Here's the point: you will likely not maintain purity in your premarital relationships if you do not let the gospel transform you in every area of life—from your views of money and time, to the way you relate to your family, to your use of your talents. The gospel must be the functional centerpiece of your life, the pivot around which the whole thing turns!

That's why we've been floating this whole topic of sexual purity on the raft of the gospel, hoping that above all we might commend the gospel to you once again. This is what good pastors do. They keep coming back to the gospel. Every week in sermons, every time they counsel a hurting person, every time they lead a meeting—it's all about the gospel. Friend, if we have done our job well, we will have given you not only a working vision of the gospel that will allow you to honor God in your dating activity but also a vision of the gospel that will help you navigate all of life for God's glory. We did not mean to be sneaky, but there you have it. Our aim in this book was to preach the gospel through the lens of sexual purity. We hope we've managed it.

In keeping with the above aim, the present chapter will begin by discussing the importance of an integrated life—one in which the gospel informs every area. Beyond this, we'll cover topics such as modesty, masturbation, flirting, entertainment choices, and use of the Internet. We believe a life where gospel purity is integrated into the whole will not only strengthen how you handle yourself in dating but will also remind you that dating is but one area of life where you are called to live before God with clean hands and a pure heart (Ps. 24:3–4).

PRE-PURITY: STARTING IN THE RIGHT PLACE

So what does a gospel-integrated life look like? What does it mean to make Jesus the hinge around which one's life turns?

First, it means we must acknowledge—indeed soulfully own—the fact that we are desperate sinners through and through. "Who can say, 'I have made my heart pure; I am clean from my sin'?" (Prov. 20:9). The answer is no one. We need grace. And how.

Second, it means we embrace the fact that we are justified before God solely on the merit of Jesus Christ, who died on the cross in our place for our sins and was raised from the dead three days later for our redeemed life (1 Cor. 15:1–3). This is not just something we believe in order to become a Christian; this must be the song of our soul, every day.

Third, it means we must ask God to convict us in the areas of our lives where grace still needs to do its work. But don't try to discover your sin all by yourself. Pray like David prayed:

Search me, O God, and know my heart!
Try me and know my thoughts!
And see if there be any grievous way in me,
and lead me in the way everlasting! (Ps. 139:23–24)

Trust us—he's better at pointing out which sins need to go, and in what order, than you'll ever be.

Fourth, it means we must realize that growth in holiness is impossible in our own strength. But what is impossible with man is possible with God. The grace that justifies us is more than mere legal cleansing; it sanctifies us as well, teaching us "to renounce ungodliness and worldly passions, and to live self-controlled, upright, and godly lives in the present age" (Titus 2:12). Seek his grace through his Word, prayer, the sacraments, and fellowship in the body of Christ, clinging to the promise that "sin will have no dominion over you, since you are not under law but under grace" (Rom. 6:14).

Fifth, and finally, making Jesus the center of your life means daily asking God for the grace of humility. Pride is the fount from which every sin flows. Pride is the lie that we don't need grace. Yet it is poverty of spirit that is the starting point of inheriting the kingdom of heaven (Matt. 5:1–3). Poverty of spirit is us agreeing with the Holy Spirit that we bring nothing but sin to God. We have nothing to commend ourselves. We need grace. That is humility. Humble people see God. Humble people see his purity. Humble people are made like him as they worship him. And humble people experience life change.

We must strive for a gospel-integrated life in which the gospel is more than a set of beliefs; it's a lifestyle. Without a doubt, this is our best defense against sexual sin. Having said the above, we are now ready to turn our attention to some other areas of life to which almost every man and woman concerned about purity should give attention.

MODESTY IN DRESS

It's beyond dispute that our society has increasingly sexualized women's clothing. So much of women's clothing today is meant to highlight—and in some sense display—a woman's sexuality. Given contemporary fashion trends, modesty won't happen without intentionality. We men, of course, need to develop the internal fortitude necessary for navigating such a sexually charged culture. And by God's grace we can. But we sure do appreciate when a woman takes care to dress in a way that honors herself and the men around her.

So, women, one way you can help the body of Christ strive for purity is by thinking carefully about how you dress. Modesty does not mean looking like an Amish milkmaid or like you were dragged through a boxwood hedge backwards. Modesty and beauty can go hand-in-hand. Indeed, some women are just plain beautiful. You could put them in a barrel and they would still be stunning. Rather, we are talking about avoiding clothing designed to highlight a woman's *sexuality*.

A key word to consider is *seductive*. When buying clothing, do you intentionally shop for outfits that are specifically designed to attract the attention of men? Are you motivated by a desire to be sexy? Do you have a specific man in mind whom you are trying to entice? If so, think twice. We're not trying to be legalistic here, but we do want you to care more about protecting the image of God within you than you care about attracting men. So be aware of your motives.

Of course, styles change. What was immodest fifty years ago might now be considered modest, given our cultural context. We acknowledge the subtleties of style and the fact that modesty can be a bit of a moving target. If you're having a difficult time deciphering whether a particular outfit is immodest or whether you regularly dress appropriately, ask an older and godly woman to help you. Ask her what she thinks about the way you dress. Ask her to go through your closet with you. Ladies, perhaps this might be a good time to take stock of your closet and to pray about editing out certain outfits. Below are a few questions to help you begin thinking about what you wear.

- Does my outfit draw overt attention to my sexuality?
- Does my outfit help protect the image of God within me?
- Does wearing this particular outfit contradict my spoken commitment to sexual purity?
- Will this outfit make it difficult for me or those around me not to "arouse or awaken love" before its proper time?

ENTERTAINMENT

Media can be a significant arena of sexual temptation. *Media*, as the word literally means, is the instrument or means for the dissemination of a thing. Much of what contemporary media disseminates is worthwhile and good. Much of it is not. Proper discernment in your media choices will help you greatly in maintaining purity with the opposite sex. Of course, there will always be a debate (among you sophisticated types, no doubt) about art versus pornography or about the extent to which sexual content in a movie can have a proper role in communicating a realistic portrayal of "life as it really is." We get that. But we are calling you to care more about your moral integrity than about your cultural and intellectual sophistication. Perhaps we sound like Shiite Baptist youth pastors, but too often we have counseled young people who can't seem to draw a logical connection between the erotic material to which they expose themselves in media and their inability to maintain proper sexual boundaries with the opposite sex.

Let's take a moment to consider three of the most powerful types of media: music, television, and movies.

Music

Our culture has replaced God's image with that of mankind's, and this is often readily seen in the secular music industry. One doesn't have to listen to the radio long in order to hear the idolatry of romantic relationships. I (Gerald) recently heard a man expressing in a love song his deep need for a woman, assuring her that if he had her love, his life would have purpose and meaning. He would not fear death, for he would know that her presence would follow him. He went on to confess that he was nothing apart from her and that her love made him whole.

It should strike us immediately that a Christian cannot truthfully sing these words to anyone other than God. The relationship between a man and a woman is meant to be the image of God's relationship with his people, but the world has allowed the image to eclipse the real thing.

If we listen closely to the lyrics of many contemporary songs, we will find that many do not speak of love and romance in ways that are consistent with the image of Christ and the church. The singers are worshiping each other rather than God. Even simple love songs that are not overtly sexual in nature are often contrary to the image God would have us display through our romantic lives. And certainly songs that celebrate premarital sex and licentious behavior obviously have no place in a Christian's life.

If we are not careful, the message of these songs will not only be implanted in our minds but also subtly imbedded in our hearts. If day after day we unthinkingly fill our minds with a message that is inconsistent with God's ideal, it is likely we will be negatively influenced by it. The messages of many songs are counter to a life of sexual and romantic purity. Are we thinking carefully enough about the message of the songs we listen to?

Movies and Television

In our contemporary culture the graphic sexual content of many television shows and movies is remarkable in scope. One wonders what has happened to our national sense of shame. Sadly, we've forgotten how to blush. And while violence as entertainment has also spiked in our culture, sex and nudity on the screen is, in our minds, more counter to God's ideal than gratuitous violence. On-screen violence is make-believe. Onscreen sex is real.

The violence we see on the screen is acting. No one is really being maimed or killed. But nudity on the screen is a different matter. When we see actors naked or scantily clad, they are not just pretending. They *really are* naked or scantily clad. Likewise, when we view a graphic sex scene, the actors are not just pretending to kiss and fondle one another; they *are* kissing and fondling one another.

It's impossible to justify viewing such onscreen activity simply because it is onscreen. If someone were to sit in a bedroom and watch a couple make love, even with their permission, we would call that person a voyeur and think his or her actions wrong. Does it make it any less wrong if the couple is on a movie or television screen?

And apart from overt sex scenes, many movies and shows are sufficiently laced with sexual content (whether it be how the actors are dressed, how they talk, etc.) that it would be impossible to edit away the inappropriate content without missing half the movie. Our desire to avoid watching such movies is not simply to avoid lusting but, rather, out of respect for the image of God that resides within the actors. Even though the actors are not respecting their sexuality, our respect for Christ should cause us to do so nonetheless. Just as we would respectfully look away from a woman whose blouse was accidentally torn, so too we should look away from a man or woman who chooses to expose him- or herself on screen. Ultimately what we value in both cases is the image of God that resides within a person's sexuality. As Christians we need to think carefully about the limits we will go to entertain ourselves.

Graphic sexual content aside, it is perhaps a bit too simplistic to restrict our viewing based on whether a certain show or movie includes a sex scene. Like we observed earlier about music, a message is conveyed with each movie and television program. As yet, evening sitcoms do not contain complete nudity. However, many shows continually portray sexuality in a way that is inconsistent with God's ideal. We must be very careful that we do not allow our desire to be entertained to overcome our desire to grow in our sensitivity toward God's truth.

It is interesting what happens when you become a parent. Suddenly the way you drive, the humor you use, and media you allow in your life all change. Why? Because now you have little ears, eyes, and hearts in your home. Even when your child is not around, you act with a new level of carefulness and discernment. You think to yourself, *What would it mean if my child knew I watched this, listened to this, or valued this*? It suggests something, we think, if we have to curtail our lives once we have the responsibility of children on our shoulders. Perhaps thinking as a parent, even before you are a parent, is a way to help think about what types of media you allow into your life. Below are a few questions to help guide your reflection on God-honoring media choices.

- Am I willing to make sacrifices for the sake of my purity, even if it means giving up my favorite television shows, movies, or songs?
- What benefits will I gain from watching these shows or movies or listening to these songs?
- What potential pitfalls might I encounter regarding my sexual purity in listening to these songs or watching these shows or movies?
- Will these songs, movies, or shows hinder my efforts not to "arouse or awaken love" before its proper time?
- Are these songs, movies, or shows creating wrong expectations for me regarding relationships with the opposite sex?

THE INTERNET

We've chosen to address the Internet separately because it has become a stand-alone media reality. In fact, movies, television, and music are becoming increasingly absorbed into the Internet. We are not far from a world where one device, with several applications, will contain our whole media reality. Access to all information is opening up to everyone, at every place, on most new technologies with extraordinary pace. Someday soon your oven will be more savvy than your current laptop.

The Internet has allowed for some pretty amazing advances, from research, to speed of access, to Bible study resources. If your pastor couldn't preach his way out of a paper bag on Sunday morning, no worries; a quick trip to the Internet gives you Martyn Lloyd-Jones to fill in the gap. But along with plugging us into the vast expanse of helpful information at lightning speed, the Internet has opened up a porthole to hell. The vast majority of pornography today is accessed through the Internet, allowing us to side-step the shame and awkwardness associated with purchasing paper porn. And the Internet preys on those of us who aren't looking for trouble. Advertisers actively go after the user, often marking our search history to help categorize and target us. This is fairly benign if we are talking about socks. But it is altogether evil when the subject is pornography and the prey is young people, even children.

We could run down the list of ways to help you remain pure in the increasingly unavoidable domain of the Internet. There are many other books and websites that can list, explain, and recommend safety nets such as filters and tracking programs.[1] Please use those resources. But you'll need more than an external hedge to maintain your purity on the Internet. If the only guardrail you have in place is an inanimate piece of technology, you're eventually going to compromise. There's just too much garbage out there, and there's no one piece of technology that can catch it all. As we discussed in chapter 5, you're going to need to develop some internal fortitude. And that only comes through real-life heart change. Find someone to pray with you, to encourage you, and to keep you accountable. And then plead with God to change you from the inside out. Be willing to take whatever measures necessary to embody his grace—even if that means unplugging altogether.

Make the gospel central in your use of the Internet. If your right eye is causing you to stumble in this area, and accountability and protective software are not helping, cut your eye out! Live without the Internet and get friends to use it for you if you ever need it. Attack the problem with earnest, blood-bought seriousness. Live a whole life—live in the integrity of purity!

Below are a few questions to consider as you think about how you use the Internet.

- How often do I find myself looking at things that cause me to stumble in the area of sexual purity?
- Have I adequately thought about whether I really need access to the Internet? Do I need it for work? Do I need to have it at home?
- Have I established proper limits for how much time I will spend online?
- Do I need to install filtering and/or tracking software on the computers I use? If so, have I?
- Do I have any people that provide accountability in my use of the Internet?
- Are the computers in my home or office set up in a place most likely to discourage improper usage?

MASTURBATION

There are various opinions among Christians on the issue of masturbation. On the whole, there aren't many Christians who aggressively advocate in favor of masturbation. There are many who are strongly against it, and then many who view it as a rather benign activity. The question thus becomes: Is there freedom for a nonmarried man or woman to use masturbation as a normal means for sexual release?

Those who are more open toward masturbation argue that, when used sparingly, masturbation can provide sexual release without becoming addictive, that sinful lust need not accompany masturbation, and that masturbation can prevent sinful lust in as much as it takes the edge off sexual buildup. And perhaps most significantly, those open to masturbation argue that the Bible is not clear enough on this issue to be dogmatic in declaring it a sin.

Those who argue against masturbation tend to focus on the Pandora's box that gets opened with masturbation—that sinful lust most often (if not always) accompanies the act of masturbation, that it often leads to frequent and addictive behavior, that it can deepen and ignite a cycle of lust and sin, and that it softens the biblical call to self-control.

We do not want to get into a pharisaical debate. And we recognize that the Bible is not explicit on this issue. Having said that, we do lean toward the "better not to go there" camp. A number of factors cause us to lean in this direction.

First, masturbation is usually born out of lustful thoughts and desires. When masturbation is done within this context, it is clearly displeasing to God. But the real sin here is the sin of lust that gives birth to, and is increased through, self-gratification. As mentioned earlier, we must learn to harness and control our sexual appetite, not arouse and express it outside a marriage relationship. Masturbation does not help foster a sense of self-control but rather short-circuits the process by which we learn to master and control our passions.

Second, masturbation is sinful when it becomes a form of sexual addiction, a way of coping with a sense of dissatisfaction in life. We cannot exist as a vacuum. We are finite creatures who long to be filled, and it is our nature to search restlessly for relief. When we are not filled with Christ himself, we will search to fill ourselves with other things. For many people, masturbation provides an immediate sense of relief from this sense of unfulfilled longing. But the relief it brings is only temporary. A prolonged addiction to masturbation can serve as an indicator that something is missing in our life. Ultimately all sins are symptomatic of a deeper issue. An addiction to masturbation is no different. The person who is addicted to masturbation is looking to meet deep relational needs that can be met only in God. Should you find yourself addicted to masturbation, more than just your behavior is the issue. It will do you little good to simply tell yourself to quit (as no doubt you've discovered). Rather, you must press toward a meaningful relationship with Christ that drives away the desire to seek satisfaction in things that can never truly deliver.

Finally, and perhaps most significantly, masturbation does not fit well with the image of Christ and the church that God intends our sexuality to portray. As we observed in chapter 1, God ordained the physical oneness of the sexual relationship to represent the spiritual oneness of Christ's union with the church. As a type, then, masturbation falls short of this reality, for it is an act that is devoid of relationship. It is using sex as a means of self-gratification apart from the gratification of another. It is an inherently self-centered affair. Sexual activity in this fashion cannot serve as an earthly type of the heavenly reality. To use our sexuality apart from the context in which God created it is to use it inappropriately. Masturbation can never be satisfying either sexually or spiritually, for it does not find its meaning in the higher reality of Christ and the church.

Is life over if you fall in this area? No. This is an area that can cause much unhealthy guilt. We certainly do not want to preach the law here. But, as pastors who love God's people, we do want to help you have a healthy, God-centered sexuality. So don't wallow in guilt, but don't be fuzzy and uncritical on this topic either.

FLIRTING

Flirting is a universally accepted form of interaction between the sexes. Even in a child's cartoon such as Aladdin, it is no big thing for the beautiful princess to bat her freakishly long cartoon lashes at Aladdin. There is even flirting in Bambi! Before you cry foul and think we are now officially getting way too horse-and-buggy on you, stay with us. We are not suggesting that there is no place for a dance of romantic interaction between two mutually attracted people. Part of a dating friendship will have this edge. But we all know women and men who seem incapable of relating to the opposite sex without flirting. What we want to warn against is a culture of flirtatiousness, where flirting becomes a normal and frequent means of relating to the opposite sex, regardless of sincerity—*serial flirting*, if you'll accept the term. Serial flirters not only flirt often but flirt with scores of different people. Here are a number of reasons we reject the culture of serial flirting so prevalent among singles.

First, serial flirting is insincere. There are healthy, God-honoring ways of making your feelings known to a member of the opposite sex. One need not adopt a passive stance under the guise of purity. (If you're passive, more than likely you're just chicken). But to carry yourself in such a way that you invite or arouse the sexual attention of every member of the opposite sex you meet is not done with a view to love and purity. Sincerity and serial flirting do not go hand-in-hand.

Second, serial flirting runs against the grain of the monogamy that will later be required in a Christian marriage. Serial flirting is a way of prematurely distributing your sexuality to many partners. This whole way of relating to the opposite sex is staggeringly offensive to the monogamy that the gospel portrays. Serial flirters often find it very difficult to cease relating to the opposite sex in this way even after they are married. That's a recipe for disaster and a deep foothold for the Devil.

Third, serial flirting often irresponsibly draws another into sincere attraction. The flirter may or may not realize this, and continue to flirt, drawing the person in more, setting him or her up for future hurt and disappointment. But, as is more often the case, the serial flirter knows exactly what he or she is doing—reeling in another person like a blue marlin, just another trophy catch. This is a terribly unloving thing to do, and yet we have witnessed Christian singles do this time and again. Flirting with anyone and everyone is nothing more than a power play and a self-absorbed quest for self-worth at the expense of others.

Fourth, as mentioned above, serial flirting is often the fruit of insecurity. The serial flirter has forgotten (or perhaps never learned) that Christ is sufficient for every need. The connection between purity and the gospel should be clear here. When someone is not secure in Christ's love, he or she often uses flirting as a means to attain a sense of worth and purpose through sexualized interaction with the opposite sex.

CONCLUSION

God is calling you to purity in every area of your life. If you're serious about maintaining proper sexual boundaries in a dating friendship, then you are going to have to be serious about maintaining purity in every area of your life. We know that many of the topics we covered in this chapter are not new. But we do hope we have connected them to a holistic portrait of purity. Strive to please the Lord with your whole life. We know you won't be disappointed.

DISCUSSION QUESTIONS

1) What topics covered in this chapter most stood out to you as areas in your life that need realignment?

2) What practical action steps do you need to put in place to realize growth in those areas?

3) Do you have other areas in your life other than your sexuality that you tend to compromise? How might getting these areas in order help order your sexuality?

9

A GOD-CENTERED VIEW OF SINGLENESS

So then he who marries his betrothed does well,
and he who refrains from marriage will do even better.
THE APOSTLE PAUL (1 COR. 7:38)

If you've tracked with the argument of this book, the following summary statement should be clear: single people are called to celibacy. Not partial celibacy, but complete celibacy. We've based this statement on the explicit teachings of Scripture (1 Cor. 7:1–9; 1 Tim. 5:2), as well as on the way Scripture reveals the typological relationship between human sexuality and the gospel (Eph. 5:21–33). God's exclusive and intimate spiritual union with the church is made known in and through the exclusive and intimate sexual union of marriage, and thus sexuality is to be reserved exclusively for marriage as a picture of this higher spiritual union.

But what do you do with all this if marriage seems an increasingly distant possibility? What if potential marriage partners are becoming as rare as the California Condor? No doubt many of our readers long to be married, but, for whatever reason, God in his providence has not provided a spouse. The sense of longing and pain many singles feel is something that only other singles can truly identify with. As Solomon says, "The heart knows its own bitterness, and no stranger shares it joy" (Prov. 14:10). We make no pretense of understanding firsthand the loneliness and pain of unwanted singleness. But we want to do our best to provide some pastoral direction in this area. God's grace is deep enough for every pain, even (especially) the pain inflicted by providence.

As we begin our discussion on singleness, we need to explode the idea that singleness is always a tragedy. Our evangelical culture generally thinks of singleness as a nonpreferred state. In fact, by many counts, a person can be classified as single only after a certain age. When you are single and in your twenties, you are thought of as a young adult. But if you are unmarried by thirty, you become officially categorized as single. Many dread the thought of that; many think it is the Death Valley of relational happiness.

But is this perspective consistent with what Scripture teaches about singleness? Not at all. As we'll see in a moment, the New Testament has a lot to say about singleness. There are two distinct types of singles—those who are single by choice and those who are not. God's Word has something to say to both groups. What's more, God's Word has something to say to those of you who think you don't belong in either group. Perhaps God is calling you to singleness. No, you say? Have you asked him? If not, read on.

SINGLE BY YOUR CHOICE

Without question, the most important passage in the Bible concerning singleness is 1 Corinthians 7:25–40. It's a long passage, but if you've never read it before, now's the time. Take a moment to consider what the apostle Paul, under the inspiration of the Holy Spirit, has to say about singleness.

> Now concerning the betrothed, I have no command from the Lord, but I give my judgment as one who by the Lord's mercy is trustworthy. I think that in view of the present distress it is good for a person to remain as he is. Are you bound to a wife? Do not seek to be free.

Are you free from a wife? Do not seek a wife. But if you do marry, you have not sinned, and if a betrothed woman marries, she has not sinned. Yet those who marry will have worldly troubles, and I would spare you that. This is what I mean, brothers: the appointed time has grown very short. From now on, let those who have wives live as though they had none, and those who mourn as though they were not mourning, and those who rejoice as though they were not rejoicing, and those who buy as though they had no goods, and those who deal with the world as though they had no dealings with it. For the present form of this world is passing away. I want you to be free from anxieties. The unmarried man is anxious about the things of the Lord, how to please the Lord. But the married man is anxious about worldly things, how to please his wife, and his interests are divided. And the unmarried or betrothed woman is anxious about the things of the Lord, how to be holy in body and spirit. But the married woman is anxious about worldly things, how to please her husband. I say this for your own benefit, not to lay any restraint upon you, but to promote good order and to secure your undivided devotion to the Lord. If anyone thinks that he is not behaving properly toward his betrothed, if his passions are strong, and it has to be, let him do as he wishes: let them marry—it is no sin. But whoever is firmly established in his heart, being under no necessity but having his desire under control, and has determined this in his heart, to keep her as his betrothed, he will do well. So then he who marries his betrothed does well, and he who refrains from marriage will do even better. A wife is bound to her husband as long as he lives. But if her husband dies, she is free to be married to whom she wishes, only in the Lord. Yet in my judgment she is happier if she remains as she is. And I think that I too have the Spirit of God.

Paul's words there tend to be a part of the Bible that many marriage-desiring singles skip right over. But we all need to consider carefully what Paul is saying here. He is not denigrating marriage. Remember, he is the same man who showed us that marriage is designed to image Jesus's relationship with the church. But here in the Corinthians passage Paul is putting marriage in its proper context. He is reminding us that marriage is only a type and shadow, a picture of a higher reality. Marriage between a man and a woman is penultimate; marriage to Christ is ultimate. As highly as Paul thinks of human marriage (and he thinks of it highly), even more highly does he think of what marriage stands for, namely, the gospel. Thus, there is a gospel calling even higher than marriage—the calling of celibacy for the sake of gospel advance.

Note in particular how Paul's awareness of the times influences his perspective on marriage and celibacy (vv. 29–31). The age in which we live is full of gospel urgency. And no one knows when it will end. Paul wants us to live in light of the pressing reality of the Lord's return. The gospel must go forth, the nations must know, and the hour draws ever closer. So the apostle says we all are to travel light. Paul knows that marriage takes energy, time, and material resources. In fact, if done well, it will take up one's life. But that means there is less energy, time, and resources to devote more directly to living strategically in this age, fully devoted to the Lord (vv. 32–35).

If the Corinthians passage is read apart from Paul's comments on marriage elsewhere, one might mistakenly conclude that Paul has a low view of marriage. But his point here is not that marriage compromises a person's relationship with Christ. Rather, he is noting the simple reality that marriage and family absorb time and energy that could otherwise be spent in carrying out the Great Commission. Of course, marriage and parenting, if done under the sovereignty of Christ's lordship, are themselves Great Commission activities. But the sort of Great Commission activity Paul has in mind here is the kind he engaged in himself—that of an itinerant missionary, who is free to travel wherever the gospel most needs to be heard. Marriage and family do not allow this sort of flexibility. It's not a coincidence that Paul, a celibate apostle, did more to further the cause of Christ throughout the Roman Empire than any of the other apostles.

Apart from the time commitment of marriage, the temporal

worries that inevitably accompany family life also tempt married folk away from an eternal perspective. Those of us who are married know exactly what this looks like. And for those of us in ministry, it's a balancing act as we try and give ourselves completely to the work of the gospel without sacrificing our spouses and children (and vice versa). Paul is challenging his readers to think carefully about the possibility of alleviating this tension by forsaking marriage for the sake of gospel advance.

The upshot is that God's Word here commends singleness as a preferred lifestyle, not simply as a fall back plan if one's hopes for marriage don't pan out. Celibacy for the sake of the gospel is not a lesser state. Indeed, if chosen for godly reasons, singleness is valuable, strategic, and commendable. This is a radical teaching, even by biblical standards. Until Christ came, singleness (and thus barrenness) in the Old Testament was considered a curse, especially for a woman. But in the new covenant, singleness is not only acceptable but also a blessed state of existence when Christ is honored as the ultimate bridegroom and where spiritual children are produced as covenant offspring by means of discipleship.[1] If what Paul is saying is true (and it is), then singleness should be something that every unmarried Christian prayerfully considers as a way of serving Christ.

SINGLE BY GIFTING

There is, however one catch to all of this. Celibacy, Paul acknowledges, is not for everyone. Those who "burn" with a strong desire for sexual intimacy should not attempt a celibate lifestyle (1 Cor. 7:9). It is better for such people to marry and fulfill their sexual passions in the legitimate context of marriage. "I wish that all were as I myself am [i.e., celibate]," Paul tells the Corinthians. "But each has his own gift from God, one of one kind, and one of another" (v. 7). Better to remain single for the sake gospel ministry, Paul says, but only if your sexual passions are under the control of a special gift.

We often hear people talk about the "gift of singleness," specifically in reference to this passage. But contrary to the way it's often stated, singleness itself is not the gift. Rather, the gift of singleness is the ability to be single and not be distressed by it. Neither of us has this gift, so we can't really tell you from experience what it's like. But if you have it, you know. Your sexual passions, while not completely dormant, do not drive your life in the same way as they do your other single friends. You want to get married perhaps, but you could be quite content to live without a spouse. Illicit sexual desire has never been a significant struggle for you. This, we believe, is a rare and special gift—a divinely given ability to live happily without the companionship and sexual gratification of marriage. If you have this gift, you need to think carefully about what you do with it. You can use it for gospel ministry, or you can use it as a means of serving yourself.

Many today, even within evangelical circles, are avoiding marriage for less than noble reasons. They don't want to spend the energy, time, and material resources that marriage demands. They want a carefree life with ample freedom to come and go as they please. Their rejection of marriage is not for the sake of gospel advance but for their own selfish ends. Singleness for the sake of self will receive no praise from God. Singleness for the sake of Christ will be richly rewarded. So, as you consider singleness, you must view it as a path of self-denial for the sake of God's glory. The life of radical discipleship is hard, no matter what road you walk.

Which path do you feel like God is calling you to? As pastors, we find it so encouraging when we see singles in our churches make wise use of their singleness. They view their singleness as an opportunity to serve Christ, and they use it well for God's glory. They are involved at church, quick to sign up for short-term mission trips and service opportunities, form thick communities, and produce spiritual children by way of discipleship. Their singleness is not a curse; it is an opportunity. Regardless of whether marriage is something they hope for or are less concerned about, they use their single lifestyle to serve Jesus. That is Paul's vision.

So consider what God would have you do with your life. Is he calling you to a path of singleness for the sake of Christ's kingdom? If you have the gift, consider well how you use it.

SINGLE BY GOD'S CHOICE

But what if you're single and don't have the gift? In nearly every respect, our contemporary culture has made life more challenging in this regard than what Paul's readers had to face. In New Testament times marriage was less about love and more about utility. It was the default setting for nearly everyone. Like getting a job, everyone got married. And like a job, some people enjoyed their marriages, and others did not. But it didn't really matter much either way. Getting married was just what you did. Your parents found you a girl from a family equal to your own, and you got hitched. Maybe you didn't marry the prettiest girl in town, but unless you came from a beggar family with no social standing or means of income, marriage was a forgone conclusion. It was just a question of who and when. But that's not how it works today.

Our culture has prioritized love over utility (which hasn't been all bad), and thus some who would have been compatible in New Testament times are not considered suitable marriage partners today. Additionally, the egalitarian nature of our society has given women a place in our culture independent of the family and home (again, not all bad). In our technologically sophisticated and relatively safe society, women no longer need a husband as they did in the ancient world. All of that to say this: our culture has made finding a spouse more challenging, and many people today are being pushed into a way of living for which they are not gifted. Being single without the gift of singleness is a tough row to hoe.

Perhaps this is where you find yourself. You deeply desire to be married. You long for the relational intimacy, partnership, and sexual union of marriage. You want to serve the Lord with everything in you, and you want a partner to do it with. But for reasons that seem beyond your control, marriage has remained elusive. And you are tempted toward bitterness and despair. Or perhaps toward foolish choices. With every wedding you attend, your suspicion that God has it in for you increases. Your angst is compounded when your friends start to have children. You have even prayed that God would help you to accept your singleness, but to no effect.

As stated from the outset, we make no pretense of understanding the relational pain that comes from unwanted singleness. But we know what it means to live with unfulfilled desires. No one gets through life getting everything he or she wants, and we are certainly no exception to the rule. And if there's one thing we've learned about disappointment, it's that peace comes only when we reckon with God's sovereignty. Rather than viewing your unwanted celibacy as rotten luck or divine punishment, we encourage you to view it as a divinely appointed fast, given to you for your blessing.

CELIBACY AS FASTING

Fasting from food is a biblically appointed means of heightening our sense of dependence on the Lord. In many respects, fasting serves much the same purpose as closing our eyes and bowing our heads when we pray. We close our eyes to eliminate distractions, and we bow our heads to remind ourselves of our humility before the Lord. Our bodily posture helps to focus our spirit. Fasting works the same way. The physical hunger that inevitably arises due to fasting serves as a bodily reminder that we are dependent on the Lord for every need. Fasting heightens our spiritual senses; it diminishes the background noise of life and brings to the fore all the things we can take for granted. It reminds us that we need God moment by moment and that it is only by his grace that we have our appetites truly filled. We say no to food in order to hunger on purpose so that our hunger can reorient us back toward God.

Yet we have appetites for more than food. Some appetites, such as hunger and thirst, are about literal survival. But there are other appetites which, while not about life and death, are an intricate part of what it means to be human—appetites for relationships, significance, purpose, and bodily comfort (to name just a few). These are good, God-given appetites. But our appetites, while legitimate, can never be fully satisfied by earthly things. The desire for a father's love can be truly satisfied only by the love of the heavenly Father. The desire for bodily comfort can be satisfied only at the resurrection of the dead, when the perishable is made imperishable (1 Cor. 15:42). The appetite for relationships—the deep desire to know and be known—can be satisfied only in the communion of the saints in glory, when the body of Christ is swept up into the divine communion of the blessed Trinity. And the desire for sexual intimacy between husband and wife can be truly satisfied only in the spiritual marriage of Christ and his church.

Our earthly appetites remind us, even when met, that something more is needed, that finite joys can never provide ultimate satisfaction. But sometimes the whole process short-circuits. The good and perfect gifts that come from our heavenly Father, and which are meant to remind us of him, become ends in themselves. We forget there is a giver beyond the gift; we forget that our appetites are meant to point us to something greater than this world can give. And so, from time to time, God will turn off the tap on one of our appetites in order to make sure we get the point. Friendship is great, but friendship with God is greater. Prosperity in this age is nice, but prosperity in the age to come is nicer. Marriage in this age is beautiful, but marriage in the age to come is more beautiful still. Just like the physical hunger of fasting turns our attention back to Christ, so too the denial of our other appetites turns us back to Christ. Sometimes God uses loneliness to get our attention. Sometimes he uses physical pain or isolation. Sometimes he denies us material blessing. These seasons of divinely appointed fasting can last for months, years, or even a lifetime. But the key in all of this is the knowledge that God seeks our blessing, not our harm. God does not take away his gifts in order to leave us destitute; he takes away his gifts in order to give us himself.

Here is the pastoral point: if you don't have a proper theology of fasting, then you are going to get upset with God when he causes one of your appetites to go unsatisfied. You will believe he is starving you. Starvation is bad. It's purposeless, harmful, and destructive. But, fasting is quite another thing. A divinely appointed fast is God's way of turning our attention toward that which truly satisfies—namely, himself. What is your view of God? Do you believe he is starving you, denying you of something you desperately need? Or do you believe he has appointed a fast for you in order to remind you that the real source of hope and joy is found in him?

Indeed, God appoints a fast for every one of his children. He disciplines us because he loves us (Heb. 12:6). If you are bearing the yoke of unwanted singleness, then trust that God has something better for you than marriage, at least for now. He's not out to rob you of joy but to lead you into it. If marriage was in your best interest, you would have been married by now. God alone knows the answer to why you are still single, despite your desire to the contrary. Rest in the knowledge that *he* knows the reason rather than in trying to figure out the reason. God has not forgotten you. The God who became man suffered, died on the cross, was buried, and then raised for you on the third day is the God who is involved in and in control of your singleness. He is involved in and in control of your sexuality. He is involved in and in control of your whole life.

So, if you are unhappily single, please remember that God is for you in Christ Jesus! Neither life nor death nor anything in all of creation—even singleness—can separate you from the love of God in Christ Jesus our Lord (Rom. 8:38–39). Yes, he knows you hunger. Yes, he knows you hunger for something good. But he has chosen, at least for now, not to satisfy your hunger, and he has done so for an infinitely good reason—that you might turn to him in deep dependence. His plan for you, for this season, is your singleness. And while he may not have granted you the gift of singleness, his grace is sufficient to sustain you through the fast. Let your hunger for marital intimacy turn your heart toward the one marriage that can truly satisfy. Friend, your singleness may be unwanted, but if you will submit to the fast, it will be a blessing nonetheless.

CONCLUSION

Living by Faith Means Trusting in the Happiness of God

I am confident of this very thing, that He who began
a good work in you will perfect it until the day of Christ Jesus.
THE APOSTLE PAUL (PHIL. 1:6 NASB)

The subject of sexuality is submerged in passion and significance. It matters a great deal to almost everyone. And the stakes are very high, not only as they pertain to our own happiness but also as they pertain to the glory and image of God. The path of the world is broad, and many travel upon it. The path of the cross, however, is narrow, and few find it. If you have become convinced of the connection between sexuality and the image of God and understand the need to direct your life away from the world's patterns, I exhort you to stand firm in the truth of God's Word. It will not be without a temporary cost, but the end for you will be blessings in both this life and the life to come.

Undoubtedly, not everything we have written in this book is wholly of God's wisdom. We trust, however, that much of what we have said is close enough to God's ideal that he will use it to assist you as you strive to live for him.

BOUNDS OF THE NEIGHBOR RELATIONSHIP

From an application standpoint, we reiterate this important truth: the bounds of the neighbor relationship are binding until marriage. If you are convinced of this singular truth, the majority of the remaining details will ultimately fall into place: dating as a category of relationship will be either abandoned or redefined, the sexual and romantic boundaries will be objectively understood, and the timing and intent of romantic relationships will be clear from the outset.

However, if you live under the mistaken assumption that a dating relationship is excluded from the biblical standard of absolute purity, you open yourself to a world of subjectivity. If you live within the clearly defined categories of the God-ordained male-female relationships, you will have the objective truth you need to live a life that honors God.

SEX, THE GOSPEL, AND THE IMAGE OF GOD: THE *WHY* OF GOD'S COMMANDS

If there is one message we have desired most to convey, it is this: sex and marriage are about the gospel. Indeed, *all* of life is about the gospel. This is the joy and hope of mankind. Everything we see, every thought we think, and every action we take should point us toward a knowledge of God. And thanks to God's Son, there will come a day when this entire world will conform to the pattern God intended. We will live in a world that conveys in all things at all times the goodness of God's glory and nature.

Sexuality is just one facet of this image. In this present life it points us toward so many aspects of God: it proclaims the hope of the gospel, speaks of our union with Christ, and reveals the goal of our salvation. Make it your goal to live out your sexuality in a way that is consistent with the image of Christ and the church. In God alone is happiness, for he is the essence of happiness itself. Trust in this happiness, for it is only when our lives are conformed to the image of this happiness that we can know true joy.

THE HOPE AND DESPAIR OF GOD'S IDEAL

Finally, the commands of God, particularly in the realm of the heart, should shatter our sense of self-sufficiency. The path to which God calls us is beyond the reach of human effort; it simply cannot be attained apart from divine assistance. Yet his commands should inspire in our hearts a sense of expectation and hope, for those commands reveal the heights to which God will take us as we look to him in faith.

We cannot live out our sexuality in a way that is pleasing to God apart from grace. And this grace is the very thing that God supplies us through Christ. Even as we finish this book, we are overwhelmed again by the standard to which God has called us in all areas of our lives and humbled by the many ways in which we seem to fall so short. But as Augustine has prayed, "Give what you command and command what you will." For the Christian, the Lord does not command that which he does not enable.

So if you find the road too long, then rest assured you have found the right road. With mankind, this journey is impossible, but with God, all things are possible. He remembers our frame, that we are but dust. His mercy and grace are sufficient for our failures along the way. Strive for the ideal with all your heart while affording yourself the same grace God has granted to you through Christ. And may we each keep our eyes on his face rather than on our own stumbling, and press on toward the goal of God's ideal. For the believer, the battle is already won; it merely remains to be fought!

BIBLIOGRAPHY

Augustine. "On Forgiveness of Sins and Baptism." In *Anti-Pelagian Writings: A Select Library of the Nicence and Post-Nicene Fathers of the Christian Church*. Edited by Philip Schaff. Edinburgh: T&T Clark; Grand Rapids, MI: Eerdmans, 1997.

Campbell, Ken, ed. *Marriage and Family in the Biblical World*. Downers Grove, IL: InterVarsity, 2003.

Clark, Jeramy. *I Gave Dating a Chance: A Biblical Perspective to Balance the Extremes*. Colorado Springs, CO: WaterBrook, 2001.

Danylak, Barry. *Redeeming Singleness: How the Storyline of Scripture Affirms the Single Life*. Wheaton, IL: Crossway, 2010.

Edwards, Jonathan. "The Excellency of Christ." In *The Sermons of Jonathan Edwards: A Reader*. Edited by Wilson H. Kimnach, Kenneth P. Minkema, and Douglas A. Sweeney. New Haven, CT: Yale University Press, 1999.

Harris, Joshua. *Boy Meets Girl*. Sisters, OR: Multnomah, 2000.

_____. *I Kissed Dating Goodbye*. Sisters, OR: Multnomah, 1997.

Holzmann, John. *Dating with Integrity*. Dallas: Word, 1992.

MacArthur, John. *The MacArthur New Testament Commentary: Matthew 1–7*. Chicago: Moody, 1985.

McDowell, Josh, and Bob Hostetler. *Right from Wrong: What You Need to Know to Help Youth Make Right Choices*. Dallas: Word, 1994.

Ortlund, Raymond C., Jr. *God's Unfaithful Wife: A Biblical Theology of Spiritual Adultery*. Downers Grove, IL: InterVarsity, 2002.

O'Brien, Peter T. *The Letter to the Ephesians*. Grand Rapids, MI: Eerdmans, 1999.

Ruppert, Martha. *The Dating Trap: Helping Your Children Make Wise Choices in Their Relationships*. Chicago: Moody, 2000.

Willard, Dallas. *The Divine Conspiracy: Rediscovering Our Hidden Life in God*. San Francisco: HarperCollins, 1998.

NOTES

Introduction

1. See Joshua Harris, *I Kissed Dating Goodbye*. Harris's *I Kissed Dating Goodbye* and his subsequent book, *Boy Meets Girl,* reject the dominant dating culture of North American Christian singles and calls for a return to courtship.

2. Perhaps the most popular has been Jeramy Clark's *I Gave Dating a Chance: A Biblical Perspective to Balance the Extremes* (Colorado Springs, CO: WaterBrook, 2000).

3. Rob Marus's "Kissing Nonsense Goodbye," *Christianity Today*, June 11, 2001, http://www.christianitytoday.com/ct/2001/june11/6.46.html?start=1.

Chapter 1: Sex and the Gospel

1. Jonathan Edwards, who saw all of earthly life as an illustration of heavenly realities, also saw marriage as an illustration of our spiritual marriage with Christ. He wrote, "[Christ is] united to you by a spiritual union, so close *as to be fitly represented by the union of the wife to the husband,* of the branch to the vine, of the member to the head; yea, so as to be one spirit." *The Sermons of Jonathan Edwards: A Reader*, ed. Wilson H. Kimnach, Kenneth P. Minkema, and Douglas A. Sweeney [New Haven, CT: Yale University Press, 1999], 186; emphasis added). Augustine also saw marriage as a fitting type of Christ and the church. He wrote, "It is of Christ and the Church that this is most truly understood: 'And they twain shall be one flesh'" ("On Forgiveness of Sins and Baptism," in *Anti-Pelagian Writings: A Select Library of the Nicene and Post-Nicene Fathers of the Christian Church*, ed. Philip Schaff [Edinburgh: T&T Clark, 1997], 39).

2. We have chosen to follow the English Standard Version's rendering of this verse, which translates the conjunction *de* ("*and* I am saying," v. 32) as "and" rather than "but" (per NIV and NASB). The point that Paul is making here is that the mystery of oneness is really about Christ and his relationship with the church even more than it is about earthly marriage. It is not as though Paul changed subjects from Christ and the church to a man and his wife but suddenly caught himself by saying, "But where was I? Oh, yes. I was talking about Christ and the church." Rather, he is trying to demonstrate that the one-flesh relationship that exists between a man and a woman (ordained in Gen. 2:24) is really about Christ and the church. In other words, to speak of human marriage is to speak of Christ and the

church. In support of this interpretation, see Peter T. O'Brien, *The Letter to the Ephesians* (Grand Rapids, MI: Eerdmans, 1999), 428–36.

3. The fact that Paul uses a passage from Genesis to refer to Christ and the church is not inconsistent with its use in its original context. Many times throughout Scripture, one verse applies to many situations. An example of this can be seen in Matt. 2:15, where the apostle mentions that Christ's journey to Egypt as a small child is a fulfillment of an Old Testament prophecy in Hos. 11:1. In the Old Testament context, the Hosea passage would have been understood as a reference to the exodus. But Matthew saw in that passage an even deeper fulfillment as it applied to Christ. Paul is using the same technique here, showing that the ultimate purpose of sex and marriage is seen with the coming of Christ. In support of this interpretation, Ray Ortlund Jr. writes, "The connective 'for this reason,' although a part of the Genesis quotation and not Paul's own insertion, gives the impression in its new Ephesians context of logical dovetailing with Paul's contextual argument" (*God's Unfaithful Wife: A Biblical Theology of Spiritual Adultery* [Downers Grove, IL: InterVarsity, 2002], 153).

4. However, even in the ancient world there was more to marriage than sex. Sex with a prostitute or a mistress did not constitute a legal marriage (e.g., see John 4:18 and the woman at the well). Along with sex, marriage in the ancient world involved a public pledge of intent, payment of a bride price, or some sort of agreement between the families of the bride and groom; only then was a sexual relationship considered to result in a legally binding marriage. Regardless, sex was still the means by which a man and woman who intended to marry actually formalized that commitment. See Ken M. Campbell, ed., *Marriage and Family in the Biblical World* (Downers Grove, IL: InterVarsity, 2003) for more information on marriage in the ancient world.

5. 1 Cor. 6:15–17 highlights this same truth as well. Just as in the Ephesians passage, Paul demonstrates here that sexual intercourse serves as a living image of our unseen union with Christ. The term "one flesh" in this passage is used to reference specifically sexual intercourse. Further, Paul's command regarding sexual purity is based on the oneness that exists in the Christian's relationship with Christ. We are called to abstain from becoming one with a prostitute because we have already become one with Christ (v. 17). We have become one with him on a spiritual plane, just as a man and a prostitute become one on a physical plane. The physical oneness then that results from sex serves as an image of the spiritual oneness that results from our union with Christ.

6. Dallas Willard makes similar critiques regarding the current evangelical understanding of the gospel in his book *The Divine Conspiracy: Rediscovering Our Hidden Life in God* (San Francisco: HarperCollins, 1998), 35–50. Though not agreeing with all of his solutions, we nonetheless affirm his recognition of the problem.

Chapter 2: More Than a Subjective Standard

1. Jeramy Clark, *I Gave Dating a Chance: A Biblical Perspective to Balance the Extremes* (Colorado Springs, CO: WaterBrook, 2000), 108–9.

2. God has not spelled out clearly why he put a decisive end to interfamily sexual relations. We are convinced, however, that this command also relates specifically to the image of God. The Old Testament law (of which the command in discussion is a part) was established as a means by which God could dwell among his people in an elevated way. Prior to the law, God did not dwell among his people in any kind of permanent capacity. The law was given that the people might know how to behave in such a way that God could live in their midst without destroying them for their sin. So through the external purity afforded by the law, God took up residence among his people in a way that he had never done before. This new relationship, in fact, served as a foreshadowing of Christ's relationship to the church. It is not a coincidence that God's commands regarding interfamily relations were given at the same time this new quality of relationship was established. Perhaps human sexuality then somehow reflects the establishment of this unique new relationship. Notice in Lev. 18:10 the reason God prohibits sex between grandparent and grandchild: "The nakedness of your son's daughter or your daughter's daughter, their nakedness you shall not uncover; *for their nakedness is yours*" (NASB). In other words, God prohibits sex between grandparent and grandchild because it is essentially like having sex with yourself. The phrase "their nakedness" at the end of this verse could refer either to the grandparent's child or directly to the grandchild. Either way, the reasoning is the same. A man's child is his very image, his own nature. So a man's child is the image of both the man and the man's father, in whose image the man was born. Thus, to have sex with one's child or grandchild is to have sex with one's own image, one's own nature. But why did God choose to prohibit uncovering one's own nakedness in conjunction with the new relationship he was establishing with his people through the law? When blood relatives come together sexually, it essentially shows the union of like natures. But when two people from different families come together sexually, it demonstrates the union of two dissimilar natures. Ultimately, then, it would seem that God has abolished sex between blood relatives because it does not portray the image of the union of two dissimilar natures, the very thing that the law foreshadowed that was fulfilled in Christ.

3. John Holzmann also argues for this standard of purity in his book *Dating with Integrity* (Dallas: Word, 1992), 79, as does Martha Ruppert in her book *The Dating Trap: Helping Your Children Make Wise Choices in Their Relationships* (Chicago: Moody, 2000), 58–60.

4. For a more detailed discussion regarding the cultural context of the New Testament, see Susan Treggiari, "Marriage and the Family in Roman Society," and David W. Chapman, "Marriage and Family in Second Temple Judaism," both in

Marriage and Family in the Biblical World, ed. Ken Campbell (Downers Grove, IL: InterVarsity, 2003).

Chapter 5: The Heart of the Matter

1. The desire that Christ is referencing is clearly sexual. When a man has sexual desire for a woman who is not his spouse, he has committed the sin of lust. We will discuss at the end of the chapter how it is possible to desire a woman (or man) as a future spouse without entering into the sin of lust.

2. See Dallas Willard, *The Divine Conspiracy: Rediscovering Our Hidden Life in God* (San Francisco: HarperCollins, 1998), 164–65, and John MacArthur, *The MacArthur New Testament Commentary: Matthew 1–7* (Chicago: Moody, 1985), 302–3. Though in our minds both Willard and MacArthur rightly capture the overall spirit of the Sermon on the Mount, they do not seem to apply its teaching consistently in the area of sexual desire. The main point of debate involves the Greek preposition *pros*, which both Willard and MacArthur translate as "with a view to," thus the translation, "everyone who looks on a woman with the intent of lusting for her." Though this is a legitimate translation, *pros* can also be used to show a close connection between things, thus the translation, "everyone who looks on a woman with regard to lusting for her." In this later translation (which I affirm), the emphasis is upon a certain kind of looking (the kind that includes sexual desire) and does not provide an exception clause if the aforementioned looking was not intentional. Even were we to grant the translation affirmed by Willard and MacArthur, it is by no means certain that Christ intended to excuse spontaneous lusting and meant to address only premeditated sexual desire. The context strongly steers us away from such a view.

3. Dannah Gresh, *The Fashion Battle: Is It One Worth Fighting?* Christian Broadcasting Network, March 1, 2004, http://theshepherdsvoice.org/news/the_fashion_battle-is_it_one_worth_fighting.html. In fairness to Gresh, the context of her statements shows that she is not trying to excuse men but to inform women of the need for appropriate dress and modesty. Though her intentions are pure, we feel that relying on this line of reasoning minimizes the power of the gospel to change a person's desires (as well as will) and neglects a positive reason for modesty. The motivation for modesty should stem chiefly from a desire to protect the image of God within human sexuality, not primarily as a means to help men refrain from lust. Even elderly women should dress modestly.

4. In the same way, even in normal, healthy marriage relationships, the stimuli required to arouse sexual desire must be increased as the relationship progresses. A prolonged kiss does not necessarily produce the same intense sexual arousal that it likely did in the early days of the relationship. Inevitably, we become increasingly aware that a sexual relationship with our spouse is not the all-satisfying answer to the ultimate longings of our soul. Prior to sexual intercourse, particularly in our

youth, we find it easy to mistakenly suppose that such an encounter will be the ultimate experience—life fully lived. But as time wears on, we realize that though the sexual relationship is filled with meaning, it cannot serve as the ultimate fulfillment of our deepest desires. It is only a shadow of the real thing. After we have drunk deeply of that cup, our perception regarding its ability to meet our deepest needs begins to become a bit more realistic. Thus, we do not gravitate toward a sexual encounter with the same intensity.

Chapter 6: Falling in Love Once

1. We have chosen to use the NIV rendering of this verse because we believe it most clearly captures the intent of the passage. The NASB, for example, translates this verse as "That you will not arouse or awaken my love, until she pleases." The NASB's translation does not seem to fit the context as readily here as the NIV. It is hard to understand why the bride would be charging the young virgins not to arouse or awaken her love, when this is exactly what she is already rejoicing in. Further, translators of the NASB added the pronoun "my" for clarification; it is not part of the Hebrew text.

Chapter 8: An Integrated Life

1. Two particularly effective web filter/tracking programs are XXXChurch.com (http://xxxchurch.com), and K9 Web Protection (www.1.k9webprotection.com).

Chapter 9: A God-Centered View of Singleness

1. A recent and compelling treatment of this is Barry Danylak's *Redeeming Singleness: How the Storyline of Scripture Affirms the Single Life* (Wheaton, IL: Crossway, 2010). We don't agree with every point Danylak makes, especially with regard to a tendency in his work to relativize marriage in light of new-covenant realities, but he does make a sound case for the new and redeemed state of singleness in the post-Pentecost era.

GENERAL INDEX

SCRIPTURE INDEX

Personal Notes

Personal Notes

Personal Notes

_____

_____

_____

_____

_____

_____

_____

_____

_____

_____

_____

_____

_____

_____

_____

_____

Personal Notes

Personal Notes

_____

_____

_____

_____

_____

_____

_____

_____

_____

_____

_____

_____

_____

_____

_____

_____

_____

_____

Personal Notes